CONT

INTRODUCTION

We all want the best for our children; above all we want them to be happy and healthy, and the food they eat plays an important part in achieving this. Our aim should be to provide our children with food that is nutritious, satisfying and fun, but this is not always easy to fit into a hectic lifestyle and a tight budget. Nowadays, we have a greater choice of food than ever before; supermarket shelves are crammed with every kind of processed food imaginable; pesticides and preservatives make it possible for fresh food to be available all year round, and the use of food additives gives us greater variety and, theoretically, greater safety. Yet, at the same time, today's parents are being warned that the types of foods many of our children eat contain hidden dangers, leading perhaps to serious illnesses in later life.

Most of us know what a healthy diet consists of: it involves eating less fat, sugar and salt, and more fibre than most of us eat at the moment. It sounds simple, but how can these ideas be put into practice, and how should we react to the recent spate of scares concerning contaminated food, the dangers of additives and chemical residues, food poisoning, lead in milk and the hazards of microwave cookers? It is not surprising that there is currently a great deal of confusion and concern amongst parents about what their children can safely eat. On top of all this, the average parent also has to cope with their own particular child's fads and fancies, and must contend with the hard-sell tactics of food manufacturers who aim their advertising directly at young consumers.

It is tempting to think (or hope) that it is all a lot of fuss about nothing. After all, most children seem healthy enough and get plenty to eat, so is there really anything to worry about? The problem is that what our children eat today could be storing up problems for them tomorrow. An unhealthy diet, with high levels of fat, sugar and salt and too little fibre, can lead to a whole host of diseases in later life – obesity, heart disease, certain cancers and tooth decay, for instance – and the rot sets in early. Just as worrying are the potential hazards of the daily cocktail of additives and pesticide residues that many children consume.

Parents want more information, yet those who ask for straight answers about the safety of food are often fobbed off with standard assurances given by the government and food industry. There is no need to despair, however. The good news is that safe and healthy eating habits established during childhood can help your child avoid diet-related diseases. The information in this book is designed to help parents make safe and healthy choices of food for their children and the rest of the family. Don't feel guilty if you can't put all the advice into practice – after all, you can only do your best to feed your child safely – but the more you can manage, the better you will all be for it.

Cook's Notes

* Recipe quantities are given in both metric and imperial. Follow one set only as they are not interchangeable
* All spoon measures are level unless otherwise stated
* For larger or smaller quantities of a recipe, simply increase or decrease the ingredients proportionally
* The number of servings given for each recipe is intended only as a guide and will vary depending on your family and children's appetites

FIRST STEPS

Breast or formula milk provides all the nutrients your baby needs for the first few months of life, but sooner or later she will be ready to start on 'solid' foods and that is when you have to start making decisions about what she should eat. Starting a baby on solid foods is an exciting time but with so much advice being pushed at parents, it is not surprising that many wonder whether they are doing the right thing, particularly when much of the information parents receive about weaning comes from baby food manufacturers who are more interested in selling their products than in encouraging parents to prepare food from scratch.

Feeding a baby should be a simple pleasure – follow this step-by-step guide and you won't go far wrong.

When to start
There is no definite time to start a baby on solid foods; what suits one baby doesn't always suit another. Most babies are ready for their first taste of solid food somewhere between four and six months. It is best not to start too early because your baby's digestive system is too immature to cope with anything other than milk or very dilute fruit juice before four months. When your baby still seems hungry after a good milk feed, or wants to feed more frequently than usual, this is often a sign that she needs more than milk to satisfy her appetite. Talk to your health visitor if you are not sure when to start, particularly if you think your baby needs solids before four months.

Introducing solid foods is a very gradual process. Eventually your baby will eat the same foods as the rest of the family, but in the early days the main aim is to get her used to new flavours and textures. Breast or formula milk will continue to provide most of the nutrients she needs for several months to come and the amounts of food eaten are so small to begin with that they make only a small contribution to her diet. Take a relaxed attitude to feeding your baby; there's never any need to rush or force feed her. If she constantly refuses food, spits it out or seems upset, don't worry, just try again another day.

Start as you mean to go on
Your baby's first foods may not provide her with a great deal of nourishment but they do help pave the way towards healthy eating habits later on. By her first birthday she will probably be eating with the rest of the family and it is far easier to establish good eating habits at the start than to try to change later. Children learn by example, so if the family's diet is basically healthy, then hers will be too. This may mean you need to make a few changes to your own eating habits and to the way you cook. In the next chapter you will find a practical guide to healthy eating for the whole family. You don't have to aim for perfection all the time – coping with all the demands your baby makes is exhausting and you shouldn't feel guilty if your good intentions sometimes fly out of the window. However, it is worth trying to establish good habits early on – they are more likely to become a way of life, and your whole family will benefit from a safe, healthy diet.

What you need
You don't need any special equipment to prepare food for your baby. Food rubbed through a small nylon sieve comes out at the right consistency but a small blender or baby mill is a worthwhile investment. A plastic bowl (one with a suction pad on the base is more likely to stay put) and spoon are best for young babies as they are simple to sterilize and won't get broken if your baby decides to throw them about!

First tastes
Ready-made baby foods may win hands down when it comes to convenience, but they are expensive and there's really no need to use them at all. Parents sometimes feel more confident that their baby is getting a balanced meal when she is given manufactured products, but home-made food is perfectly safe, nutritious and quick to prepare, and the big advantage is that you know exactly what your baby is getting.

Kitchen hygiene

Your baby can easily pick up infections so pay particular attention to hygiene when preparing her food.

＊ Wash your hands before handling food or feeding equipment. Once your baby starts feeding herself, get into the habit of washing her hands too.

＊ Dishes, spoons and feeder cups harbour germs so sterilize them regularly by immersing in sterilizing solution and rinsing in boiled water before use. You should do this at least until your baby is about seven months old but, even when she's older, it's still important to keep things scrupulously clean.

＊ If you use cans or jars of baby food, remove just enough for your baby's meal. The remainder can be covered and kept in the refrigerator for up to 24 hours. (Food from cans should be transferred to a clean bowl first.)

＊ Throw away any leftover food – it may be contaminated with bacteria from your baby's mouth.

＊ Food cooked in advance should be cooled quickly and refrigerated or frozen until required. Reheat it really thoroughly, then let it cool down to the right temperature for your baby.

＊ Boil tap water before using it for drinks or reconstituting food until your baby is about eight months.

Using mostly manufactured foods may result in your baby becoming so used to their flavour and consistency that she will be reluctant to eat ordinary family foods later on. Try to keep packets and jars for when you are in a hurry, out for the day or just too exhausted to prepare food from scratch. Bulk cooking and freezing of foods like fruit, vegetables and soups saves time and means there is always something handy when time is short – simply cook, purée and freeze in ice-cube trays, then pack into freezer bags. This way you can pop out tiny portions whenever they are needed.

Around four months Start with fruit or vegetable purée (such as potato, carrot, cauliflower, banana, apple or pear) or sugar-free baby rice mixed with a little breast or formula milk. Just a teaspoon or two at one feed is enough, along with the usual milk feed. It is often better to offer some of the milk feed first until she is used to taking food from a spoon; if you don't you are likely to end up with a screaming hungry baby who refuses even to try the new food. Offer the food from the end of a small spoon so she can learn to suck it off. It will take time for her to learn this new skill, so don't be disappointed if progress is slow. Be patient and don't spend a lot of time trying to persuade your baby to eat if she's not interested. Once she gets the hang of things, try giving her a little solid food at two feeds, then three, gradually increasing the quantity.

By about five months You can increase the variety of foods you give your baby. Start to include foods like meat, fish, poultry, beans and lentils, but don't be tempted to give too much variety too quickly. Three or four new foods each week is about right. Don't add salt to food, even if it tastes bland, because a baby's kidneys are not mature enough to deal with a lot of salt. Steer clear of sugar and sugary foods, too, because babies are quick to acquire a sweet tooth. Avoid wheat cereals (containing gluten), citrus fruits, nuts, ordinary cow's milk and eggs until six months because they can trigger allergies in some babies.

By six months Babies can eat most foods providing the consistency is right, that is it is still sieved or puréed, with no lumps. At this stage you will be able to use most of the foods the family is eating, which makes life much easier for you and gets your baby used to eating the same as everybody else. Milk is still important but your baby will gradually need less. Once a reasonable amount of food is being eaten, try giving cooled boiled water or *very* diluted fruit juice at one meal instead of milk, and try giving some drinks from a spouted cup. Be guided by your baby – if she still wants a milk feed with every meal, let her have it.

At this stage you can switch to ordinary cow's milk (there's no need to boil it unless it's the unpasteurised, green-top kind) but it's preferable to stick to breast or formula milk until a year old. Use whole milk until your child is at least two years old. Skimmed and semi-skimmed milks don't contain enough energy or vitamins for very young children. Providing your child is eating a good variety of foods you can switch to semi-skimmed milk once she is two. Skimmed milk is fine from about five.

Bought baby foods – are they better than home-made?

Commercially produced baby foods make up a substantial part of the average British baby's diet. In 1988 babies ate their way through over 90 million tins alone and, despite scares about the contamination of baby foods with bits of wire and glass, sales are soaring. One reason for this is that many anxious parents lack confidence in their own ability to provide the 'right' food for their baby.

Commercial foods certainly *seem* to have a lot to rec-ommend them: They are quick and convenient, appear to offer lots of variety and claim to be hygienic, safe and nutritious, but there's absolutely no *need* to use them at all. For some parents, using tins, jars or packets of baby food is the answer to the problem of what is best for their baby, especially as most of the literature about feeding babies that is available in hospitals, clinics and 'bounty' packs comes from baby food manufacturers. However, such literature contains little advice for parents who want to prepare food from scratch, promotes the use of commercial baby food and is often accompanied by free samples.

The content of commercial foods varies with the brand and product. Although there is usually plenty of information on the pack, it is not always clear and can be misleading. Take a look at the ingredient list on a can or jar of a savoury meal, for example – water is often the first ingredient on the list

Goat's milk and soya milk drinks are sometimes given to babies who are allergic to cow's milk, but it's important to talk with your doctor or health visitor first as these milks lack certain important vitamins and minerals.

From about seven months Encourage chewing by giving lumpier food, even if there is no sign of any teeth! If you continue to purée everything, your baby may learn to prefer sloppy food and refuse anything remotely lumpy long after she's perfectly able to cope with it. Try mashed or minced food instead of puréed, but don't worry if she gags or refuses at first – simply try again a few days later. Even if your baby doesn't like lumpy (which means the food contains more of that than anything else), and it is usually impossible to tell exactly how much meat or vegetables it contains. Packs do give nutritional information, but many omit to give details about how much sugar is in the product. Even products which claim to be low in sugar or sugar-free may actually contain sugar in less-easily recognised forms, such as glucose, fructose, syrups, concentrated juice or honey. Unfortunately, all these are just as harmful to babies' teeth.

Manufacturers often draw attention to the fact that their products are free of additives, such as colouring, artificial sweeteners and flavour enhancers. These claims are usually perfectly true, but such substances (except for three vitamins used as colourings) are banned from *all* baby foods, anyway. Few baby foods are made from organic ingredients and levels of pesticide residues in these foods have been found to be higher than previously thought. (The government is currently taking steps to reduce pesticide levels in baby food.)

On the positive side, some manufacturers have reduced or removed sugar from baby food and are ensuring their foods are tamper-proof by using special seals. Cans or jars of instant food are fine occasionally – if you are in a hurry, out for the day or just too exhausted to prepare something from scratch – but try not to rely on them as a regular part of your baby's diet. If you do buy commercial foods, look for varieties that are free from added sugar, such as pure fruit, vegetables, sugar-free baby rice and cereals.

food she'll probably enjoy gnawing at 'finger' foods, such as chunks of peeled apple, carrot, fingers of toast or sugar-free rusks (see recipe on page 50). Avoid sugary foods like biscuits and sweet rusks (even so-called 'low sugar' rusks can contain as much as 15 per cent sugar) as they encourage a sweet tooth and may lead to tooth decay later. Give her a spoon to hold so that she can join in at mealtimes. It's great fun, but be prepared for the mess by spreading some newspaper or a plastic sheet under the highchair. Take comfort in the fact that she'll find her mouth sooner or later.

By nine months to a year Your baby's mealtimes will probably

Top tips for feeding your baby

✶ Don't be in a rush to introduce solid foods – most babies are ready for their first tastes of food at around four months, others are happy with breast or formula milk until about six months. Talk to your health visitor or clinic if you think your baby needs solids before four months.

✶ Try to give plenty of variety – eating a varied diet is the best way to ensure your child gets all the nutrients she needs. Aim at a reasonably healthy diet right from the start.

✶ Avoid adding sugar to your baby's food. Limit sugary foods like biscuits, jam, ready-made desserts, cakes, sweets and soft drinks. Even products claiming to contain 'no added sugar' may contain other forms of sugar, like glucose, fructose or honey, which are just as harmful to teeth.

✶ Avoid wheat, citrus fruits, cow's milk, egg and nuts until your baby is six months old. Egg white is best avoided until about eight months. All eggs should be *thoroughly* cooked.

✶ Don't add salt to your baby's food. Cook family foods without salt and add it after you have removed your baby's

---

coincide with the rest of the family. Once she can chew well, simply chop food into small pieces.

Extra vitamins

Providing your baby is eating a good variety of foods she shouldn't need extra vitamins, but as a safeguard the Department of Health recommends that drops containing vitamins A, C and D be given to babies from six months until at least two years, and preferably until the age of five, particularly if a child is fussy about food. Babies occasionally need vitamins earlier than this – sometimes from as young as a few weeks old – but your doctor or health visitor will advise you when to start. Vitamin drops are available from your clinic and are an inexpensive way of giving your baby the extra vitamins she needs. Follow the directions on the pack and don't be tempted to give more than the recommended daily dose.

portion, if necessary.

✻ After about six months, include fibre in the form of whole grain cereals, such as wholemeal bread, whole grain breakfast cereals (Weetabix, Ready Brek or porridge, for example), fruit, vegetables, pasta and rice. Never add bran to your baby's food and avoid bran-enriched foods.

✻ Stick to breast or formula milk for the first six months and preferably until a year. Ordinary whole cow's milk can be given to babies from six months. Skimmed milk is not suitable for the under-fives (it lacks important vitamins and energy) but you can introduce semi-skimmed milk from the age of two, providing your child is eating a good variety of food. (Stick to whole milk if your child is faddy.)

✻ Never add cereal to your baby's bottle.

✻ Avoid small hard food which can cause choking. Whole peanuts are not suitable for children under five.

✻ Give vitamin drops from six months to two years. If your child is a poor eater, continue until she is five.

✻ Never leave your baby alone when she is eating or drinking.

My baby won't eat!

Weaning a baby doesn't always go smoothly. Some babies don't seem to enjoy eating at all, others will only eat a few foods, find lumps impossible to cope with or eat everything on offer, only to be sick a few minutes later. Most parents come up against some sort of feeding problem from time to time. It's difficult not to feel concerned, but the best advice is not to worry and to try to relax – the majority of problems do sort themselves out. Providing your baby is healthy and gaining weight normally there's usually nothing to worry about. Having her weighed regularly will put your mind at rest, but if you really think there's a problem, ask your health visitor or doctor for advice.

Baby drinks – the best choice for your baby

It's a big moment when your baby is ready to try something to drink other than milk or boiled water, but when it comes to choosing that new drink the huge selection on offer can be

Top tips for baby drinks

✳ Breast or formula milk is the best choice for babies until a year old, but cow's milk can be given from six months.
✳ Milk, water or well-diluted fruit juice are best for older babies and toddlers.
✳ Never add sugar to drinks for babies and children.
✳ Check ingredient lists to see exactly what drinks contain. Even 'no added sugar' or 'low sugar' drinks may contain sugar in one form or another.
✳ Avoid giving drinks containing sugar (remember even pure juices contain natural sugars) in reservoir feeders or for long periods from a bottle. Limit them to mealtimes.
✳ Start giving some drinks from a spouted cup once your baby is about seven months old.
✳ Boil and cool ordinary tap water or filtered water until your baby is about eight months.
✳ Don't give bottled water to very young babies or use it to make up feeds.

confusing. The sugary drinks and syrups that once dominated chemists' shelves are disappearing, but are the new generation of baby drinks any healthier and are they really necessary?

Breast- and bottle-fed babies don't usually need extra drinks during the first few months. (Give cooled boiled water if she seems thirsty between feeds.) However, when you start introducing solids, and your baby starts drinking less milk, you might start considering other drinks to satisfy her thirst. There are plenty of drinks to choose from, many claiming to be designed specially for babies.

Cow's milk You can switch to ordinary cow's milk once your baby is six months old, but breast or formula milk is the *best* choice for babies until their first birthday.

Follow-on milks These are sold as powder for reconstituting with water and claim to be designed specifically for babies over six months who are eating solids. They are *not* a substitute for breast or formula milk for younger babies. Although follow-on milks have more vitamin D and iron than ordinary cow's milk,

16

there are no real advantages in using them, because once your child is eating solids she can get all the nutrients she needs from food and her usual milk. Follow-on milks are an expensive and unnecessary way of buying milk.

Baby fruit juices and drinks

Fruit juices and drinks made specially for babies are a popular choice, but the confusion starts when you are faced with interpreting the descriptions on the packs. There is a big difference between *fruit juice* and *fruit juice drink,* even though they are sold in similar packs. Descriptions like 'sugar free' and 'low sugar' can be misleading too, so scrutinize labels before you buy. Many of these drinks claim to be suitable for babies from four weeks, but it's best not to introduce them until later.

Pure unsweetened baby fruit juices are 100 per cent juice, with no added sugar or other sweeteners. They are sold ready to drink in small cartons or bottles, or as concentrates (which may contain added preservatives) that need diluting with water. Although they are a reasonably healthy choice, they tend to be more expensive than ordinary juice and have no real advantages. Dilute well and keep for mealtimes.

Baby fruit juice drinks are not the same as pure fruit juices. The concentrated type (for diluting with water) contain some fruit juice but they also contain water and added sugar – either ordinary sugar (sucrose) or other forms like glucose syrup. Ready-to-serve fruit juice drinks sold in cartons or bottles also contain some fruit juice but you can end up paying for a lot of water (sometimes as much as 80 per cent) as well as juice, and they usually contain sugar in one form or another.

Instant baby drinks are sold as dried granules or powder that you mix with water. What you end up with is sweetened water flavoured with very small quantities of herb extract. Despite claims on the packs, there is no evidence that these drinks have a soothing effect on babies.

Ordinary unsweetened fruit juices are 100 per cent pure fruit juice with no added sugar or additives, though some may have added vitamin C.

Best for baby There's little doubt that frequent sugary drinks and syrups can cause tooth decay, which is why many manufac-

Water, water everywhere – but is it fit to drink?

Doubts over the quality of drinking water have prompted many people to switch to bottled waters, but beware if you are thinking of giving them to very young babies. Although they are pure water, some contain high levels of mineral salts which can put a strain on a baby's immature kidneys. Don't be tempted to use them for making up milk feeds – if you want to introduce them, wait until your baby is well established on solids and eating a good variety of foods.

Although tap water is safe to drink, there is increasing concern over its quality and the levels of some substances it contains, such as nitrate and lead. Water filters reduce levels of some of these substances in water and can be an inexpensive way of improving what comes out of the tap. Filtered water can be given to babies and children but most manufacturers recommend that it shouldn't be used for making up feeds. Filtered water should be boiled and cooled for babies under eight months.

turers have reduced or removed sugar from drinks designed for babies. Even so, we can't afford to be complacent: pure fruit juices with no added sugar still contain natural sugars and most baby drinks (even those claiming to be lower in sugar than other brands) contain up to 10 per cent sugar (either natural sugar or a mixture of natural and added). As far as your baby's teeth are concerned, it doesn't matter which type you give your baby; what's more important is how often your baby has them and what she drinks them from. Frequent sugar-containing drinks (including juice) do more damage to teeth than when they are given in one go at mealtimes. They are particularly harmful in reservoir (dinky) feeders and bottles used like a dummy because the teeth are bathed in sugar for long periods.

The best drinks for your baby and toddler are milk and water. Give well-diluted fruit juice (ordinary juice works out cheaper than baby juice) for a change at mealtimes.

SAFE AND HEALTHY EATING IN CHILDHOOD

Once you have got through the weaning stage, your child will be eating much the same food as the rest of the family. This is the time when many parents find themselves increasingly concerned about what their children are eating – not just about the amount of fat and sugar in their diet, but also about the safety of food and ingredients and other issues. As children get older, particularly when they go off to school, they start making some of their own decisions about what they eat, so how can parents ensure their children will make the best choices? Read on and you will find out how to give your child a safe and healthy diet and establish good eating habits that will set them up for life.

What do children need?
Children need food to fuel and nourish their bodies. Growth and development is a demanding business, needing large amounts of energy and nutrients. Children may be small but their requirements are high – they actually need the same amounts of some nutrients as adults. Requirements vary at different ages but charts with details of how much protein, energy, vitamins and minerals children need are not much help to the average parent trying to feed a family. If anything, they cause anxiety that your child may be going short of important nutrients when, in fact, there's usually nothing to worry about.

The key to a healthy, nourishing diet is variety – much easier to remember and put in practice than long lists of nutrients. Variety means giving your child a good range of foods over the course of a week or so. That way you can be pretty certain she will get all the nutrients she needs. The variety of foods you give should include plenty of healthy choices. Although lots of different processed fatty or sugary foods may be considered a varied diet, it's the wrong type of variety.

Aim to give some foods from each of the following categories over the course of a few days:

✻ fruit (or fruit juice) and vegetables
✻ meat, fish, poultry, eggs or pulses (beans, peas and lentils)
✻ milk, cheese, yogurt or other dairy foods
✻ bread, cereals, rice or pasta
✻ fats like polyunsaturated margarine and oil (only small quantities are necessary)

Don't worry if your child goes through stages of refusing all but a few foods; just try to encourage as much variety as you can manage, even if it means eating the same variety day after day.

Healthy eating for children – why bother?

Experts agree that a healthy diet means eating less fat (particularly saturated fat), sugar and salt and more fibre, but is there really any need to encourage children to eat a healthy diet? What your child eats today, and the eating habits she learns during childhood, could be storing up trouble for tomorrow. Unhealthy diets are related to a whole host of diseases – obesity, heart disease, certain cancers and tooth decay, for example. The rot sets in early: 50 per cent of children have dental decay before they even start school, and the build-up of fat on artery walls that can lead to heart disease can start well before children reach their teens. The most recent government survey of schoolchildren's eating habits revealed just how appalling the diets of some youngsters really are (see opposite).

Healthy eating – what the experts recommend

Eat less fat, particularly saturated fat Some fat is essential. It supplies fat-soluble vitamins, and certain types of fat are vital for growth and development. However, too much fat in the diet can be unhealthy. Fat and fatty foods are high in calories and can contribute to overweight. Diets high in fat are also associated with serious diseases, like coronary heart disease and certain cancers. Fats can be divided into three basic types – saturated, monounsaturated and polyunsaturated. Too much saturated fat, in particular, is associated with an increased risk of heart disease because it tends to increase the amount of cholesterol in the blood, which leads to a build-up of sludgy deposits on artery

The diets of British schoolchildren – a cause for concern

Different children eat different foods, but the most recent government survey into the diets of British schoolchildren (undertaken in 1983 but not officially published for over six years) reveals a far from healthy picture of what many are eating. The survey's main findings were:

* around three-quarters of children ate more fat than levels currently recommended; a quarter ate particularly high levels of fat

* some children, especially girls, had intakes of calcium, iron and certain vitamins (A, D and B$_2$) below recommended daily amounts

* older children who ate out of school at lunchtime (at cafés or fast food outlets) had lower intakes of many nutrients than other children; in particular girls' diets were short of iron

* many children's diets were heavily dependent on chips, biscuits, meat products, cakes and biscuits; older children in particular ate a lot of fat in the form of chips

* chips, buns and pastries dominated the weekday lunches of many schoolchildren

Although the report found little evidence to suggest that children were suffering from these apparently unhealthy and deficient diets, it's an obvious cause for concern and a good reason for encouraging healthier eating habits in your own child.

walls, eventually causing the blockages responsible for heart attacks and strokes. Although coronary heart disease is rare in children, the gradual build-up of cholesterol on artery walls can start well before the teenage years. Monounsaturated fats have little effect on blood cholesterol levels; polyunsaturated fats may actually help to lower them.

Eat less sugar Sugar is not essential but is hard to avoid altogether because it is hidden in so many foods. Sugar provides calories, but no other nutrients, and too much can lead to overweight. Sugar is also a major cause of tooth decay. All sugar is damaging to teeth, particularly when it comes in sticky forms like cakes, biscuits and sweets. The more often it is eaten, the more harm it does. Frequent sugary snacks are far worse than the same amount of sugar eaten in one go.

Eat less salt For some people, too much salt can lead to high blood pressure, which in turn increases the risk of heart disease and strokes. While there's still disagreement about the effects on health of too much salt, most experts believe that the evidence is sufficient to recommend a reduction in salt intake.

Eat more fibre Fibre plays a vital role in keeping our bodies healthy, but it may seem odd that something with no nutritional value should be so important. As well as helping to prevent constipation, fibre also appears to protect us against diseases like bowel cancer and even heart disease. Fibre is a mixture of different substances and most fibre passes through the body unchanged. The various types of fibre appear to play different roles in preventing disease. Adding bran to everything isn't the best way of boosting fibre intake (too much bran can reduce the absorption of important minerals) but eating more unrefined, starchy foods like wholemeal bread and whole grain cereals, along with plenty of fruit, vegetables and pulses, will ensure a healthy intake of the various types.

Do healthy eating guidelines apply to children too?

Although it's agreed that recommendations for healthy eating apply to adults and children over five, there are currently no official recommendations for the under-fives. Good eating habits should be encouraged as soon as babies start on solid foods, but whether very young children should consume relatively low-fat, high-fibre diets is a controversial issue. In general, the guidelines *do* apply to children of all ages, but because young children have high energy and nutrient requirements and aren't capable of eating large amounts of food, it's important that they have full-fat dairy foods, such as whole milk and cheese, until the age of two. Too many bulky, high-fibre foods should also be avoided because very young children may find it difficult to eat enough food to get all the nutrients they need. Once your

---

The habits of a lifetime

From an early age, children are beginning to form the eating habits of a lifetime. Good, healthy eating habits will ensure that your child is well nourished and will help her avoid diet-related diseases later on. The earlier she learns them, the more likely they are to become a firmly established way of life. It also means that when your child starts making her own decisions about what she eats she's more likely to make healthy choices. Establishing good eating habits doesn't mean scrutinizing every mouthful your child eats, but it is worth making her diet as healthy as possible right from the start. Making sure the whole family's diet is healthy will automatically ensure your child's is too.

---

child reaches two, and providing she's eating a good variety of foods, you can *gradually* change from whole milk and other full-fat dairy foods to lower-fat alternatives (but steer clear of skimmed milk until she's five), and gradually include more fibre-rich foods.

Safe and healthy eating

Putting all the theory about healthy eating into practice may seem daunting, but it's far easier than it sounds and well worth the effort. It may mean making changes to the meals your family eat and the type of foods you buy. The weekly dash around a busy supermarket with young children in tow doesn't give harassed parents much time to compare different products, and even when labels do include nutritional information it's not always easy to understand them. Making a list of what you want to buy may help to make it easier.

If you think you need to make changes to the way you shop and eat, don't try to do it all at once. Make changes gradually – perhaps buy some extra fruit or vegetables one week or switch to wholemeal bread another, or try making a meal a bit healthier by using less fat or adding more vegetables or pulses, for example. If you rely heavily on convenience foods to save time, there

Coping on a small budget

Feeding a family on a small income can be a nightmare, particularly if there are other problems, such as not having proper cooking facilities, or being miles from the nearest shops. Growing children need nourishing food and can have large appetites, but food isn't cheap and money doesn't always stretch far enough. The type of food that experts recommend for a healthy diet and what you can actually afford may seem poles apart.

If you're struggling to feed your family on a small amount of money, don't feel guilty if you think you can't afford to make changes. Just aim to give a reasonably varied diet and your child should get the nutrients she needs. Highly processed foods tend to be expensive for what you actually get, but basic foods like bread, cereals, pulses, milk, baked beans, potatoes, rice and some vegetables contain a good range of nutrients, are healthy and more affordable. Meals for the whole family can be nutritious and economical – home-made macaroni cheese, flans, jacket potatoes, pizza and shepherd's pie, for example. Less expensive meatless meals (see page 109) are just as nutritious as those containing meat.

Make sure you are receiving all the income support and benefits you are entitled to – your children may be entitled to free school meals, milk and vitamins, for example. Ask for advice at your local Social Security Office or Citizens' Advice Bureau.

are plenty of healthy foods to choose from and many of the recipes in this book are designed to be quick and easy (see page 100).

Healthy eating and shopping needn't cost more. Trying to feed a hungry family on a low income can be a nightmare and it's a sad fact that foods like wholemeal bread, polyunsaturated margarine and lean meat cost more to buy, but this can be compensated for by spending less on processed foods. Highly processed foods are often an expensive way of buying basically cheap ingredients and nutrients – weight for weight, the fish you get in fish fingers, for example, is more expensive than buying ordinary fresh or frozen fish. Basing meals on cheap, nutritious foods, such as pasta, rice, pulses, bread and vegetables, can actually mean you spend less than if you buy a lot of processed foods.

Simple guidelines for healthy eating

Follow the suggestions overleaf and you should automatically provide a healthy diet without having to spend a lot of extra time or money. Remember you are only trying to do your best – don't feel guilty if you can't manage everything.

Perfect pearlies – how to prevent tooth decay

Almost 50 per cent of pre-school children have tooth decay and over 90 per cent of fifteen-year-olds have at least five decayed teeth, yet tooth decay is almost entirely preventable. Help keep your children's teeth in top condition by following these simple rules:

✱ Eat less sugar. Sugar is a major cause of tooth decay – frequent sugary snacks do more damage than the same amount of sugar in one go, so keep sweet treats and sugary foods for mealtimes. If your child wants a snack between meals, choose something that is healthy and low in sugar.

✱ Fluoride can help protect against decay by strengthening tooth enamel and making it more resistant to attack. In some areas, fluoride occurs naturally in the water, and in others it is added to drinking water supplies by the water authority. If you live in an area where the drinking water doesn't contain fluoride, you can give your child drops or tablets. (To be really effective, give them from the age of six months to 12 years.) Ask your dentist for advice.

✱ Clean your child's teeth and gums *thoroughly* every day (after breakfast and at night) with a fluoride toothpaste and a well designed child's toothbrush.

✱ Make sure your child has regular dental check-ups.

Making sense of food labels

Reading food labels can help you make healthy choices and compare different products. However, while the information on packs must be true, at present it is sometimes given in a confusing way or may lead consumers to believe they are buying products which are healthier or more beneficial than they really are. Bear this in mind the next time you look at food labels.

All food must be marked with its name or description. Most pre-packed foods must also give a list of ingredients in order of weight, the name and address of the manufacturer or seller, along with a 'sell-by date', with keeping times or a 'best-before date' and any special storage or cooking instructions. In addition you may find:

Nutritional Information Information on the nutritional content of food is not yet compulsory (except on foods which make specific nutritional claims), but an increasing number of manufacturers now give a nutritional breakdown of their products, including the amount of calories, fat, saturated fat, protein and other nutrients they contain. Despite the existence of the government's voluntary code for nutritional labelling,

* Eat fewer fatty foods, such as processed meat and meat products (burgers, sausages, tinned meat, pâté), full-fat dairy foods (cream, ice-cream, full-fat cheese), pies, pastries and savoury snacks. Eat less butter, block margarine, suet and blended vegetable oil, all of which are high in saturated fat. Switch to polyunsaturated margarines and oils (labelled 'high in polyunsaturates') but don't eat too much of these either.

* Eat fewer sugary foods, such as cakes, sweets, biscuits, jams, ready-made desserts and soft drinks. Reduce the amount of sugar you add to food in cooking and at the table.

* Eat fewer salty foods, such as processed meat, savoury snacks and salted foods. Add less salt to food.

* Eat more fresh vegetables and fruit, bread, potatoes, pasta and rice (wholemeal if possible), pulses (beans, peas and lentils),

this type of information is given in different ways by different manufacturers, which can make it difficult to compare products. Sometimes the information isn't in a particularly useful form either – for example, the label may often give a figure for the total amount of carbohydrate contained, but that figure includes both healthy starches *and* not-so-healthy sugars.

Claims about the nutritional or health values of food
Although these must be truthful, they don't always tell the whole story:
'No added sugar' – but the product may actually contain sugar in other forms, such as glucose, fructose, syrups or honey, all just as harmful to children's teeth
'Low sugar' – means there's some sugar. If other forms of sugar are also present the overall sugar content could actually be quite high.
'No artificial sweetener' – but there could still be a lot of sugar or other sweeteners
'No artificial additives' – but natural additives may have been used instead. Natural additives sound more wholesome but some are extracted from insect shells and bird feathers
'High fibre' – but containing a lot of fat or sugar as well

whole grain breakfast cereals (low-sugar or sugar-free, such as Weetabix, Shredded Wheat, porridge oats, instant oat breakfast or puffed rice), lean meat, poultry and fish.
* Choose healthy alternatives to what you already eat – semi-skimmed milk (once your child is two), reduced and low-fat cheeses, canned fruit in juice rather than syrup, wholemeal bread instead of white, sugar-free jams, diluted juice instead of squash, and food without unnecessary additives like colourings.
* Choose healthier types of convenience food (see page 28).
* Although the occasional packet of sweets, crisps or savoury snacks won't do your child any harm, they provide little more than calories and are low in nutrients. There is no need to ban them altogether, but keep them to a minimum. If your child wants a snack between meals there are plenty of healthy alterna-

tives – small savoury sandwiches, bread sticks, home-made pop-corn, fruit, vegetables, cubes of cheese, low-fat yogurts, milk or diluted fruit juice are popular with most children.

✳ Look at the labels on manufactured foods – they may not always give you much information but can give you clues about what they contain (see pages 26–27).

Safe and healthy cooking

Make the most of the food you buy by preparing and cooking it in the healthiest way:

✳ Wash fruit and vegetables really well. Peeling removes pesti-cide and other chemical residues which may be present on the skin, but it removes some of the fibre too.

✳ Grill, bake, stir-fry, poach, steam or boil instead of roasting or frying.

✳ Trim off any visible fat from meat and reduce the amount of fat you add to food in cooking. Skim the fat off casseroles, soups and stews.

✳ Cut down on the sugar and salt you add to food; use alterna-tives like herbs.

✳ Use less meat; buy smaller amounts of lean meat and add more vegetables or pulses to make it go further.

Healthy convenience foods

Many parents find the idea of coping without convenience foods hard to contemplate. There is no doubt that convenience foods can make life easier, but unfortunately many of them are high in fat, sugar, salt and additives – the very things your child is better off without. Moreover, it's often impossible to know exactly what convenience foods contain – a 100 per cent beef burger, for example, can legally contain over 10 per cent water and up to 35 per cent added fat, but there's no way of knowing this from the label. When buying convenience foods, it is all too easy to end up paying a lot more for basic ingredients, such as meat, because they are bulked out with cheap ingredients.

There is nothing wrong with giving your child highly processed convenience foods occasionally, but a diet of burgers and chips day in, day out won't do her much good. Over three-quarters of the food we buy is processed in some way, but that doesn't automatically mean it is bad for your children. Fortunately, some convenience foods actually fit in neatly with ideas about healthy eating so when you reach for something quick and easy, try to choose healthier alternatives. Healthy convenience foods include:

✱ frozen fish, fruit and vegetables

✱ pizza (some have a wholemeal base, but check ingredient lists for unnecessary additives like colourings)

✱ canned fish, beans, fruit in natural juices and vegetables like tomatoes – look for those with no added salt, sugar or colouring

✱ yogurt – natural and sugar-free are the best choice

✱ fish fingers (but check the ingredient list carefully – look for those with fish as the main ingredient and with no additives like polyphosphates and colourings)

✱ breakfast cereals (low or no-sugar varieties)

✱ many basic foods can be used as 'convenience' foods because they are quick and easy to prepare – fresh and dried fruit, bread, jacket potatoes, easy-cook pasta and rice, nuts and beans

It's never too late to make changes
As parents get the message about healthy eating, more want to make changes to the type of foods their children and the whole family eat. It's never too late to start making changes and even if your child has grown up as a junk-food addict so far, there's a lot you can do to improve her diet. Use the guide to healthy eating on pages 26–28 to make changes, but don't try to do everything at once – your child and the rest of the family are more likely to accept changes if you introduce them gradually.

Overleaf is a list of the changes that one family made. Before the changes, the children were eating a lot of saturated fat, sugar and additives and not much fibre. Afterwards, the whole family had a much healthier diet and enjoyed the food just as much.

Before	**After**
Breakfast	
sugar-coated cereal	whole grain breakfast cereal
toast and butter	toast with polyunsaturated margarine
fruit squash or tea	fruit juice diluted with water
Lunch	
packed lunch of luncheon meat sandwiches, crisps and a chocolate biscuit	packed lunch of wholemeal sandwiches with canned fish or egg, fresh fruit and a fruit yogurt
can of fizzy drink	
Dinner	
fish fingers and chips	fish fingers, peas and jacket potato
ice-cream and canned fruit in syrup	canned fruit in fruit juice with yogurt
Snacks	
packet of sweets	nuts and raisins
biscuits	fresh fruit

Making food fun

Making your child's food fun and enjoyable to eat is just as important as making it healthy. However nutritious food is, it's only good for your child if it gets eaten. Appearance is important, particularly to younger children.

There's no need to turn every meal into a masterpiece but a bit of imagination can make all the difference. Children have fewer chances to learn about food and healthy eating at school, so encourage them to help at home. They will enjoy learning about healthy food and ingredients, and are more likely to eat something they've helped to prepare. Try some of the following ideas:

✻ Use a few bits of fruit or vegetable to make faces on top of casseroles, pies and quiches – use slices of tomato or carrots, peas or beans for features like eyes and mouths, and grated carrot or cress for hair.

✳ Use a sharp knife or some novelty biscuit cutters to cut out shapes from foods like bread, sandwiches, cheese, raw vegetables and fruit.

✳ Make home-made jelly in tiny jelly moulds. If you occasionally buy yogurts or other ready-made puddings with children's characters on the pots, keep the pots to put your own desserts in.

✳ Make pictures with food; arrange food on a small plate to look like a face, train or other shape.

✳ Young children like individual foods – a tiny bread roll, mini sandwich, tart or cake, or a salad or some fruit in a small cake case is often more appealing than a serving from a large dish.

✳ Involve your children in preparing food – let them help with jobs like sifting flour, beating eggs, stirring ingredients or rolling out pastry. Give them a small piece of dough or pastry to make their own little loaves or pies.

Drinks for toddlers and older children

Squashes and other soft drinks may not be thought of as suitable for babies but they are popular with older children. Unfortunately, many contain little more than sugar and water along with a hefty dollop of additives, such as colourings, flavourings, preservatives and artificial sweeteners. While concentrated citrus fruit *squashes* must have at least 25 per cent real juice, concentrated fruit *drinks* need contain only 7 per cent fruit, and that includes pith and peel as well as juice. Ready-to-serve fruit juice drinks and fruit *flavoured* drinks must contain some juice (though you usually end up paying for a lot of water and sugar, too), but fruit *flavour* drinks don't have to contain any fruit or real juice whatsoever.

Water, milk or diluted pure fruit juice are the best choice for older children. If they insist on soft drinks, scrutinizing the list of ingredients will give you some idea of what the various drinks contain. Some manufacturers have removed unnecessary additives (such as the colouring tartrazine) from soft drinks. High juice squash contains more actual juice than standard squash, and tends to be lower in additives, but it is still high in sugar. Sugar-free soft drinks won't damage your child's teeth, but most contain little or no real juice and a number of additives, such as artificial colourings and sweeteners.

31

The most recent arrivals on the soft-drinks' shelves are squashes and drinks with added vitamins and minerals. Don't be fooled into thinking they are any better for your children – the sugar they contain is still just as harmful to teeth.

Off to school

Providing a healthy diet for pre-school children is a relatively easy affair because what your child has to eat is largely up to you. Once your child goes off to school, however, things can change dramatically. You have less control over what your child eats and, for older children in particular, what they choose to eat during the day becomes their own affair.

School meals – good, bad or non-existent?

In the past, if your child stayed to school lunches, you could be reasonably sure she was getting a decent meal. Until 1980, legislation ensured that school meals prepared by local authorities met specified nutritional standards, providing, amongst other things, a third of the energy and 40 per cent of the protein requirements of children. Since then, however, guidelines for the nutritional content of school meals have been abolished. Schools are now under no obligation to provide meals at all, except to children whose families receive income supplement. Many schools who continue to provide meals have switched from the traditional meat-and-two-veg approach to cafeteria-style meals with more emphasis on fast foods. In this type of system, children are free to make their own choices about what they eat, some children ending up with a well balanced healthy meal, while others choose chips, doughnuts and squash – a meal high in fat, sugar, salt and additives, and a far cry from the type of healthy eating being advocated for children.

Fortunately, school meals are improving again, with some schools and local authorities laying down good nutritional standards for meals, and encouraging children to make healthy choices. However, in the absence of national standards for school meals it is largely a matter of chance what your child is given for lunch. There is growing pressure for the re-introduction of nutritional standards, so if you're dissatisfied with the type of food on offer at lunchtime, encourage your child's school to make changes towards healthier meals. Ask the PTA or parent-governors' association to act on your behalf, or write to the head teacher or local education authority.

If it looks as though no changes will be made, encourage your child to make the best of what is on offer. She stands the best chance of being able to do this if she has learnt good eating habits from an early age. If you are still unhappy about what she gets to eat, or the school has stopped providing meals, the best alternative is a packed lunch. At least you will know what your child is eating and you can make it as healthy as possible. On page 91 there are lots of ideas for healthy packed lunches.

Extra vitamins – do children need them?

A healthy diet with plenty of variety should provide babies and children with all the vitamins they need, but the huge number of vitamin supplements on sale for children is enough to make any parent feel their child may be missing out on something important. So how can you ensure your child gets an adequate intake of vitamins, and are supplements really needed?

The amounts of vitamins needed for healthy growth and development are tiny, but children do have relatively high requirements. Breast or formula milk should provide most babies with all their essential vitamins during the first few months of life, and the various meals and snacks eaten by toddlers usually add up to a well-balanced diet with plenty of vitamins. Even toddlers who are hell bent on avoiding all but a few foods actually seem to manage to get an adequate intake of vitamins. According to most experts, vitamin deficiency almost never occurs in babies and children in the UK, but there are exceptions:

✻ Some Asian children develop rickets due to an extreme lack of vitamin D

✻ Premature and low-birth-weight babies may have increased requirements for vitamins

✻ Young children drinking goat or soya milk may not get an adequate intake of vitamin B_{12} and folic acid

✻ Vegan children may be at risk of vitamin B_{12} deficiency

Ask your doctor or health visitor for advice if you think your child is at risk of deficiency. (The government is currently revising their recommended daily intakes of vitamins for children.)

Will extra vitamins boost your child's brainpower?

If you read recent reports that extra vitamins might boost children's scores on IQ tests, or improve difficult behaviour, perhaps you were tempted to give supplements to your own child. Before you dash out and clear the shelves of vitamin pills, remember that the majority of experts remain sceptical. Studies suggesting that vitamins can boost brain-power are far from conclusive. What they do show, how-ever, is just how bad some children's diets really are, and that better eating habits would ensure adequate intakes of all vitamins. The best advice is to ignore unproven claims about the health and other benefits of supplements for children and to concentrate on encouraging healthy eating habits that will automatically ensure your child gets an adequate intake of all the vitamins and other nutrients she needs. Giving your child vitamin supplements won't do any harm (although large doses of some vitamins can be dangerous) but they're unlikely to make her any brighter or healthier and are usually a waste of money.

Toddlers and the under-fives Most healthy, well nourished toddlers and youngsters don't need extra vitamins, but as a safeguard it's worth continuing with the vitamin drops rec-ommended for babies (see page 14) until your child is two, and preferably until the age of five if she's fussy or faddy about food. **Older children** Supplements should not be necessary for older children at all, but the most recent survey of schoolchildren's eating habits showed that the unhealthy diets some children consume may be deficient in certain vitamins. Although vitamin supplements might help balance things up a bit, they are not the best answer to unhealthy eating habits. If you ensure your child eats a basically healthy diet, with plenty of variety, she'll automatically get a plentiful supply of vitamins. There's no need to ban unhealthy foods like chips, crisps and sweets altogether, but don't let them take the place of more nutritious foods on a regular basis.

Make the most of vitamins

Bad storage, preparation and cooking can destroy or reduce the vitamin content of food. Follow the tips below and you'll be making the most of vitamins naturally present in food.

∗ Look for food that is in good condition. Fruit and vegetables that have been lying around for days on end will contain less vitamin C than those that are really fresh. Store fruit and vegetables in a cool, dark place and prepare them just before they are needed. Keep milk out of direct sunlight to preserve its riboflavin content.

∗ Keep losses to a minimum by cooking fruit and vegetables as quickly as possible in a small quantity of water, or by steaming. Overcooked fruit and vegetables that are left standing around for ages before being eaten will have lost most of their vitamin C. Fruit and vegetables cooked in a microwave retain slightly more vitamins than those cooked conventionally. Best of all, eat raw fruit and vegetables whenever possible – they're richer in vitamins and children often prefer them to the cooked variety.

Vitamin-enriched junk food – trick or treat?

Food manufacturers haven't been slow to exploit parents' concern about their children's diets. The potential profits in vitamin-enriched foods aimed largely at children are enormous. Some manufacturers are adding vitamins to junk food like crisps, ice lollies, instant desserts, sweets and squash, but does it really make them any better for your children? The simple answer is no. Vitamins or not, these foods tend either to be made from ingredients with low nutritional value, or else the processing involved in their production destroys the natural vitamin content. Don't be conned into thinking the added vitamins in these foods turn them into something healthy or superior – many still contain high levels of fat, sugar, salt and additives and are low in fibre. Your child is better off without them and better off getting the vitamins she needs by eating a healthy diet and healthier snacks instead of lots of junk foods like crisps, sweets and squash.

Food additives – a cause for concern?

Providing a healthy diet for children isn't all that worries parents today. Rumours about the possible dangers of chemicals used in food production, or additives put in during processing, have led to increasing concern about the safety of foods. According to some press reports, even basic foods like fruit, vegetables, meat and milk may not be as healthy as we are led to believe.

The use of food additives has risen rapidly with the introduction of modern food processing techniques. Over 3,500 additives are currently used in food. Some have an important function (helping to preserve food, for example) but the majority are used for purely cosmetic reasons, making food look and taste better than it would without them. Since 1986, all additives, except flavourings, have been declared in the list of ingredients on packaged foods. Additives have to be declared by their name or number, including an 'E' prefix if they have one. 'E' stands for EEC and means the additive is one of the 150 or so substances regulated by the EEC. Additives without 'E' numbers are allowed in the UK but may not have been passed for use throughout Europe. Most food sold loose (bread, cakes, pies and meat products, for example) doesn't have to declare which additives it contains, or need give only limited information, so there's no way of knowing what you're getting.

Should your child avoid additives?

Opinion about the safety of food additives varies. The food industry and government maintain that additives are perfectly safe, but some experts aren't convinced, believing that certain additives could be putting our children's health at risk. It is known that some children are intolerant to particular additives, and hyperactivity in a very small number of children has been linked with additives like tartrazine (a yellow food dye).

Although it is generally agreed that the risks to health of eating additives are extremely small, it does seem sensible to avoid them whenever possible, particularly as the long-term effects of consuming a daily cocktail of additives simply aren't known. The average child in the UK consumes around 2 lb (1 kg) of additives a year, and foods like soft drinks, savoury snacks, sweets and instant desserts (which are marketed directly at children) are often high in additives. Some manufacturers are voluntarily removing colourings and other additives from processed foods, but check the ingredient list to see exactly what you're buying. Don't assume that natural additives are automatically a better, safer choice than artificial ones – some manufacturers have replaced artificial additives in some foods with natural ones simply to be able to make the claim that there are no artificial additives in the food.

Eating a healthy diet with plenty of fresh foods and fewer highly processed ones will automatically keep the level of additives your child consumes to a minimum. The London Food Commission has drawn up a list of additives which are known or suspected of carrying risks to health. This is currently being up-dated but the LFC can be contacted for advice on additives (see page 156).

Hidden 'additives' – pesticide and chemical residues
Some of the pesticides and other chemicals used during food production leave residues, but their use doesn't have to be declared. A billion gallons of pesticides are sprayed on to fruit and vegetables every year, fertilizers are used routinely, antibiotics may be used to produce meat, fungicide is used on citrus fruit after harvesting, and fish and chicken feed may contain colouring to improve the colour of farmed fish and eggs. Consumers are given reassurances that these substances pose no threat to health, yet a recent scare about the possible link between cancer in children and Alar (a growth regulator used in apple production) shows just how worried parents are becoming. (The manufacturers of Alar have since withdrawn it, for the time being.) Even if consumers want to avoid food treated with chemicals, it's virtually impossible to do so because information about the use of chemicals in the production of certain foods is not available.

Keeping additive and chemical residue intakes to a safe minimum
* Eating a healthy diet with plenty of fresh foods and fewer processed foods will automatically ensure your child gets the nutrients she needs, and keep her intake of additives and chemical residues to a minimum. A good diet will help to keep your

child healthy and her body will be able to cope with these substances when she does eat them.

✳ Scrutinize ingredient lists and choose foods which are free from additives or have only short lists. Some additives make food appear more nutritious and wholesome than it really is, so check the small print to see exactly what you are buying. Manufacturers are beginning to remove at least some unnecessary additives from processed foods so, if you do buy them, compare brands and choose those with the least additives.

✳ Don't assume that natural additives are automatically better than artificial ones – all additives are best kept to a minimum.

✳ Fruit and vegetables may contain pesticide and other residues but the advantages of eating them as part of a healthy diet outweigh the disadvantages. Wash all fruit and vegetables *really* well. Peeling will remove chemical residues left on fruit and vegetable skins (although it won't remove those which are distributed throughout the food).

✳ Buying organic food is one way of avoiding chemical residues. Organic produce isn't cheap but perhaps you could afford some – that way you'll be casting a vote for safer food. Accept the fact that organic produce may not look as uniform as mass-produced food but it's better for you.

✳ Consumers have a right to know whether food contains additives or chemical residues and should have greater access to information about the safety of these substances. All food (prepacked and loose) should be properly labelled. If you feel strongly about the use of these substances in food, want better labelling or greater openness about their safety, make your views known (see page 41).

Food poisoning – how to ensure your child's food is safe
The number of food poisoning cases has risen dramatically over recent years. Although most cases are relatively mild (causing stomach upsets and diarrhoea for a day or two), some types are serious and babies and young children are particularly vulnerable. Various incidents have hit the headlines – salmonella in eggs and poultry, listeria in chilled ready-made meals and cheese, and botulism caused by contaminated yogurt. So how can you be sure that the food you buy for your children is safe?

Food poisoning results from eating food contaminated with

harmful bacteria or the toxins they produce. The bugs that cause food poisoning are sometimes present in very small numbers in food and can be eaten without ill effects, but under the right conditions (when there's food, moisture and warmth) they can multiply to levels that cause food poisoning. Cool temperatures below 5°C don't kill bacteria but do slow down their growth (except listeria which thrives even in refrigerated food). Thorough cooking destroys bacteria, but it doesn't destroy the toxins and spores made by some types of bacteria.

The foods most likely to cause food poisoning tend to be high in moisture and protein – cooked meats, poultry, ready-made meals, prepared salads, eggs and egg dishes (particularly those containing raw or partly cooked egg) and dairy products, for example. Food may have been contaminated during production and food poisoning often results from subsequent poor food hygiene, bad storage or cooking – either by food manufacturers, retailers or consumers. To avoid the risk of food poisoning, follow this simple guide:

✻ Buy food in good condition from a reputable store with good hygiene standards and a fast turnover of food. If in doubt, don't buy.

✻ Check the 'sell-by' or 'best-before' date on packaged food. Don't eat food beyond the recommended period after the sell-by date and throw away food after the best-before date.

✻ Get chilled and frozen food home as quickly as possible and store it properly immediately. Delays (especially in hot weather) could allow the temperature of the food to rise and food poisoning bugs to multiply.

✻ Store foods at the correct temperature and check any special storage instructions on packs. Some foods, such as long-life milk, fruit juices, mayonnaise and reduced-sugar jam, need refrigerating after opening.

✻ Avoid rusty, leaking, badly dented or blown cans. Wipe the tops of cans before opening. Treat canned food as fresh once it has been opened. Store leftover canned food in a clean bowl in the refrigerator.

✻ Food cooked in advance should be cooled rapidly, covered and refrigerated. Don't reheat food more than once.

✻ Keep your refrigerator clean and run it on the lowest setting, but not so low that food freezes.

∗ Wash your hands before handling food. Raw food can contaminate cooked foods, so wash your hands and utensils between handling raw and cooked food, and store raw and cooked or ready-to-eat foods separately to avoid any cross-contamination.

∗ Keep your kitchen clean, especially surfaces or utensils used for food preparation.

∗ Cook eggs, poultry and meat really thoroughly.

∗ Wash salads in running water.

∗ Some chilled ready-made meals are infected with food poisoning organisms such as listeria, so it's essential to store them properly and reheat really thoroughly. Never just warm them up. Take particular care when reheating foods in a microwave cooker (see below).

∗ Soft unpasteurised cheeses, such as Brie and Camembert, can contain high numbers of listeria and are best avoided by pregnant women (because of the risk to the unborn child), babies and people who are ill.

Is microwave cooking safe?

Microwave cookers are ideal for busy parents because meals can be ready in minutes, but you could be putting your family at risk of food poisoning. Recent reports have suggested that microwave cookers may cook food unevenly so that parts of the food (usually the centre) do not reach a sufficiently high temperature to kill off food poisoning bacteria. The main concern is about food known to be contaminated with bacteria, particularly chilled ready-made meals (an estimated 25 per cent of which are contaminated with listeria) and poultry. Microwave instructions aren't always given on these foods, leaving it up to the consumer to guess whether they are suitable for cooking in the microwave and how long to cook them for. The government has recently reported on the efficiency and safety of microwave cookers and around a third of microwave cookers failed to pass the government's tests, that is they failed to heat food evenly to a high enough temperature to kill harmful bacteria. Follow these tips to ensure the food you cook is safe to eat.

∗ If there are no microwave instructions on packs of prepared food or meals, assume that they are not suitable for cooking in a microwave. Don't cook chilled ready-made meals in a microwave unless clear instructions are given by the manufacturer. Even then, it is safer to use your conventional oven.

* Thaw frozen cooked foods thoroughly before reheating.

* Food positioned towards the outer sides of a microwave cooker cooks more quickly, so place thicker pieces of food around the edge of dishes.

* Stir foods whenever possible during or after cooking.

* Don't reheat very large pieces of food (whole or large joints of poultry, for example). Cut food into smaller pieces and turn or rearrange during cooking.

* Reheating times will vary depending on the power output of your microwave. Check your cooker manufacturer's handbook.

* Make sure food is piping hot right through. As a guide, it should be too hot to eat when it first comes out of the cooker. If possible, use a food thermometer to check the food is at least 70°C, and preferably 80°C, throughout. Even if food is bubbling around the edges, don't assume it's cooked right through.

* Standing times are very important as they ensure food is completely cooked.

* Don't reheat babies' bottles in a microwave cooker – hot spots can result in burns. Recent research has given rise to a concern that heating baby (formula) milk in a microwave can result in the production of potentially harmful substances. Although this has yet to be confirmed, it is another reason for *not* using your microwave cooker to warm your baby's bottle.

* Keep your microwave really clean.

Making your voice heard – getting the food you want
Parents expect the food they buy to be safe and nutritious, but recent food scares have raised doubts about the safety and wholesomeness of food. Consumers look to the government (in the future they'll look increasingly to the EEC) to set and maintain food standards, to prevent them being deceived or offered poor quality food and, above all, to protect them from hazards. Yet confidence in the government as guardians of food quality and safety is at an all-time low. We're all free to choose what our children eat but, in order to make the safest and healthiest choices, we need open and honest information about the food we buy. The confusion created by conflicting opinions about

Irradiated food – would you give it to your child?

Food irradiation is being hailed as one way of reducing the risk of food poisoning, but would you buy irradiated food for your child to eat? Over 25 countries already permit the process and the government are planning to lift the current ban on food irradiation in the UK. It has been claimed that consumers will benefit from safer, better-quality food and less wastage, yet there's growing concern about the less desirable effects of irradiation and the abuses that may occur.

Food irradiation involves treating food with gamma rays. Pre-packed food receives a measured dose of radiation. This causes chemical and biological changes that kill bacteria, moulds and pests, inhibits sprouting in vegetables and delays the ripening of some fruits. Food doesn't become radioactive, but the process extends the shelf-life of food, is claimed to reduce hazards (such as salmonella) and eliminates the need for certain food additives and chemicals.

Although the government and some food manufacturers are convinced of the benefits of irradiation, most consumer groups are concerned that the process could bring new problems for consumers. The main concern is that there is no test

food safety and the current lack of openness and information means parents are often unable to weigh up the risks.

Parents want less secrecy and more information. They want to know, for example, whether food additives and pesticide residues pose a threat to their child's health, how food has been produced and exactly what it contains and how nutritious it is.

If you are concerned about the food you buy, don't be afraid of asking for changes or more information. Too often decisions about food production and content, and the policies that determine it, are taken without asking consumers what they really want. The more pressure put on by consumers, the more likely things are to change. If you are unhappy about the food on offer or want more information, write to food manufacturers, retailers to detect whether food has been irradiated or re-irradiated, or to check the process has been carried out properly. Evidence that food has been correctly irradiated will depend on manufacturers' records, and the absence of a suitable detection test could lead to the misuse of irradiation to clean up contaminated foods. Cases of this hazardous practice have already hit the headlines with reports of food that has been rejected as unfit for consumption being irradiated and offered as fresh and wholesome. The problem is that irradiation doesn't destroy bacterial toxins and spores which could lead to serious health problems. There is also concern that the process could reduce the nutritional value of foods or produce potentially harmful substances in it.

Providing food irradiation is carried out properly, it does have potential benefits, but it seems strange that a process which can't be detected and could lead to abuse is being permitted. Some major food manufacturers and retailers say they will not stock food that has been irradiated, and many retailers and consumer groups are opposed to its introduction. Whether or not irradiated foods actually end up on the supermarket shelves remains to be seen – whether it ends up in your shopping basket is up to you.

and your MP or MEP. Let them know what you think about food and what you want. Groups such as The London Food Commission and Parents For Safe Food are committed to getting a better deal for consumers. They believe that we all have a right to good-quality, unadulterated, affordable food, and that the addition of unnecessary substances to food and the use of unnecessary processes should be minimised. They put pressure on the government and food industry for, amongst other things, better access to information about food, better food laws and labelling to protect consumers. Help them if you can by joining or supporting their campaigns (see page 156).

FEEDING PROBLEMS AND SPECIAL DIETS

Fussy eaters – coping with a child's wayward appetite
For many parents, worrying about which foods their child should be eating isn't the problem – actually getting their child to eat anything at all becomes the major issue. For these parents, trying to impose recommendations for a healthy diet on a child's wayward appetite becomes almost impossible. Don't despair if your child's mealtime mutiny means all your good intentions fly out of the window. Mealtimes needn't become a battle of wills and you can rest assured that your child is unlikely to come to any harm.

Feeding problems are very common in young children. In fact, the majority of parents come up against some sort of problem related to eating at some time. Problems occur in children of all ages and for various reasons, but toddlers are notorious for suddenly refusing certain foods (usually the healthy ones you want them to eat) or eating hardly anything at all. The average faddy eater simply won't eat what her parents want her to at a particular time. Others will happily eat a certain food one day and refuse it the next. Feeding problems in young children occur for various reasons, but they often start when a child is trying to establish her role within the family. Young children depend on their parents for their wellbeing, but also have a strong need for independence, and mealtimes are often when children choose to challenge the expectations of their parents by being fussy or faddy about what they eat. Although food fads are usually only a passing phase, it's difficult not to feel concerned or upset. Most parents find it hard to believe that their child can survive on so little food and that she will eventually eat normally, but the problem almost always passes with time.

Will a faddy child end up malnourished?

No child will allow herself to starve, and refusing to eat rarely results in a child becoming malnourished. Most children eat when they are hungry and, over a period of time, even the most fussy eaters manage to get a reasonable balance of nutrients.

Babies and toddlers grow very rapidly in their first year, but their growth rate slows down during the second year and children often start to eat less. A one-year-old who eats well may be extremely finicky at two, and mothers often remark that the baby seems to eat more than the toddler. Growth occurs in spurts and it's normal for children to eat more at some times than others. Children can be perfectly healthy on remarkably little, and providing your child is healthy and growing normally there's usually nothing to worry about.

How to cope

If you're up against a feeding problem, try not to let it get you down. It's worth remembering that feeding problems are very common and can occur at any time in childhood. Concentrate on what your child will eat rather than what she won't and don't worry too much, for the time being, about making her eat foods you think are healthy. If your child refuses to eat them she can get the nutrients she needs from other foods. Aim at giving as much variety as you can (even if it's the same variety everyday) and make any snacks as nutritious as possible, such as fruit, wholemeal sandwiches, and so on. Some foods that parents think of as essential for children (meat or eggs, for example) don't actually need to be eaten at all and the stangest choices of food can provide children with a perfectly healthy diet.

Children tend to eat when they're hungry and are often better at coping with several small meals or snacks than a large amount of food in one go. Try to keep mealtimes relaxed and positive. Don't waste time and energy trying to force a child to eat; mealtimes fraught with anxiety will make your child even less likely to eat. Simply put the meal before your child without fuss and clear it away without comment if she doesn't want it. Let her see the rest of the family enjoying food and leave it at that.

Having your child weighed regularly will reassure you that she's growing normally, and you'll be less likely to push her to

Top tips for coping with a faddy eater

✱ Food fads are almost always a passing phase. Don't force your child to eat or turn mealtimes into a battle of wills. Bribing, coaxing, pressurising or punishing your child are unlikely to solve the problem and may make it worse. Tension is likely to put her off eating and makes mealtimes a misery for you and your child.

✱ Try putting less on your child's plate. A pile of food can be off-putting to young children, especially if you argue about how much of it has to be eaten. A tiny portion that's eaten happily is better than nothing at all and you can always give more if your child wants it.

✱ Concentrate on what your child *will* eat. Don't spend hours preparing something you know won't be eaten. Stick to simple things like bread, cheese, baked beans, yogurt and fruit, for example – you'll feel less resentful if it ends up in the bin. Make food look attractive – a bit of imagination can make a lot of difference to youngsters. Bits of fruit and vegetables are ideal for making faces on food, and novelty cutters transform things like bread, fruit, vegetables and cheese into food that's fun to eat (see page 30).

✱ Your own attitude to eating will be passed on to your child, so set a good example at mealtimes and your child will eventually do the same.

✱ Don't worry too much about providing healthy food for

eat when she's not hungry. If you are really worried it's worth keeping a diary of everything your child eats over several days. You may well find that she's eating more than you think, or it could be that she's having so many biscuits and drinks that there's not much space left for other food at mealtimes. If you still think your child's eating habits are more than just a passing phase, ask your doctor or health visitor for advice.

Food fads are far less common in older children, although some remain fussy throughout childhood. Older children often the time being. The strangest combinations can provide enough nutrients, and children can be perfectly healthy on remarkably little. Just aim at giving as much variety as you can manage. Sooner or later she'll want to try other foods but this might not be for a long time.

* Remember that no normal child will allow herself to starve. If your child is healthy and growing normally it's a sure sign that she's getting the nourishment she needs.

* Keep a record of everything your child eats over a few days – she's probably eating more than you think. If you're still concerned, talk with your health visitor or doctor.

* Involve your child in preparing part of the meal (washing fruit and vegetables, mixing ingredients, laying the table, for example) – that way she's more likely to try something. Let her serve herself if possible.

* Try limiting less nutritious snacks like biscuits and sweets in between meals but bear in mind that several small meals or snacks suit some children better than larger meals. Make sure any snacks are as healthy and nourishing as possible.

* Keep mealtimes calm, relaxed and positive. Talk about things other than food. Even if your child doesn't eat much you'll feel less frustrated and angry. Encourage her when she does eat but don't go over the top with praise. Eating with other children can sometimes help. If you know a child who's a good eater it may be worth asking him or her to lunch or tea.

have strong views about the types of food they want to eat (often the result of hard-sell advertising by food manufacturers). A compromise is the best approach – don't force your child to eat something she really dislikes and let her have foods that she likes but ensure she has a reasonable variety of healthy ones too – that way she'll get the nutrients she needs. It won't happen if she eats too many foods like crisps, chips, biscuits and sweets, so aim to keep these to a sensible minimum.

Coping with special diets and disabilities

Coping with children on special diets or with feeding difficulties can cause a lot of worry and concern, especially in the early days. Conditions like diabetes, coeliac disease, food allergies and intolerance, phenylketoneuria or less common metabolic disorders all require special diets – usually for life. Some parents are faced with the problems of feeding children who are mentally or physically disabled or born with conditions like cleft palate which can make feeding difficult until things have been corrected. Coping with these types of problems can seem daunting, particularly in the early days, but help is at hand. Your doctor, health visitor or dietitian will be able to give you help and advice. You can also turn to organisations and support groups – they're not an alternative to medical advice but do give practical help and support to parents (see pages 153–156).

The vegetarian child

The number of vegetarians in this country has increased rapidly in recent years and many parents are opting to bring up their children as vegetarians. Most vegetarian parents know by experience what makes a healthy balanced diet, but problems arise when children from meat-eating families suddenly become vegetarian. According to the Vegetarian Society, there's a growing number of children who, while their parents remain contented carnivores, decide meat is definitely not for them. With under-fives, it's rarely because they associate meat with the animal it came from; some babies simply seem to have a genuine dislike of all things meaty from the first mouthful. Toddlers are also notorious for going through stages of refusing to eat certain foods, including meat. Although this faddy phase is usually short-lived, a young child's refusal to eat meat sometimes becomes a permanent habit. Older children who decide not to eat meat don't usually change that decision. Often what makes them change to a vegetarian diet is the discovery of where meat really comes from or the facts behind factory farming, and they invariably have strong views on the subject.

Are vegetarian diets safe for children?

Whatever the reason for a child not eating meat, coping with a vegetarian child in the family can cause anxiety. Many parents worry whether meatless meals will be nourishing enough for growing children. Scares that children eating wholefood diets may become malnourished (so-called 'muesli-belt malnutrition') have caused unnecessary concern about vegetarian diets. Experts agree that vegetarian diets can be perfectly nourishing for babies and children of all ages. In fact, there's plenty of research suggesting that this type of diet is actually healthier than a meat-and-two-veg approach to eating. Vegetarian children tend to eat fewer fatty and sugary foods and more whole grain foods, fruit and vegetables, which fits in neatly with ideas about healthy eating and means they are less likely to suffer from diet-related diseases like obesity, heart disease and tooth decay.

Obviously it's important to know what your child should be eating instead of meat and fish. Variety is the key to a nourishing vegetarian diet. Vegetarian children can get all the protein and other nutrients they need from mixtures of grains or seeds with pulses (beans, peas and lentils) or nuts – beans on toast, peanut butter sandwiches or macaroni cheese, for example, are excellent sources of protein for growing children. Most vegetarian children eat eggs, milk and other dairy products, too, which bumps up protein and nutrient intakes even further. It's true that the levels of some vitamins and minerals are lower in plant foods, or less well absorbed by the body, but eating a wide range of foods ensures a plentiful supply. There's no need to fork out on vitamin supplements, but do give the usual vitamin drops until your child is at least two years old (see page 14). Vegans, who exclude all foods of animal origin from their diet, are usually advised to take a supplement of vitamin B_{12}.

All the basics of a healthy vegetarian diet, such as pulses, nuts, rice and cereals, are available from supermarkets and most food shops, as are time-saving convenience foods like cans of beans, pizzas, vegetarian burgers and sausages. Eating away from home may be more of a problem – check what's on offer at your child's school or nursery; a packed lunch may be the simplest solution.

Ask your health visitor for further advice or contact the Vegetarian or Vegan Societies who both provide a range of useful information about feeding children (see page 155).

FIRST FOODS

Once the initial weaning process is over, babies can eat most foods and family meals from about six months, providing the consistency is right (that is, puréed, with no lumps to choke on) and salt and sugar are omitted. Remember to avoid ordinary cow's milk, eggs, citrus fruits, nuts and spicy food until your baby is six months old (see page 14). When you do introduce eggs, make sure they are always *thoroughly* cooked.

Many mothers like to cook individual meals for their baby at first, particularly if she eats at a different time of day from the rest of the family. The recipes that follow are quick and easy to prepare, make baby-size portions and are just as nutritious as anything you will find in a packet or jar. All the recipes can be made in advance and kept in the refrigerator for up to 24 hours; some are also suitable for freezing. Avoid adding salt or sugar and remember to reheat food thoroughly and allow to cool to the right temperature before giving it to your baby. Once your baby starts eating lumpier food, simply mash or mince food instead of puréeing it.

Plain Rusks

These are a healthy, sugar-free alternative to manufactured rusks which can contain as much sugar as sweet biscuits. (Even so-called 'low sugar' rusks may contain up to 15 per cent sugar.) Cut thick slices of wholemeal bread (about ½ inch/1 cm thick), cut off the crusts and slice into fingers about 1 inch (2.5 cm) wide. Place on a baking sheet and bake in the oven at 140°C (275°F) mark 1 for about 40 minutes or until dry and crisp throughout, turning two or three times during cooking. Store in an airtight container for up to a week.

Finger foods

Somewhere between nine and 12 months, your baby will start to enjoy feeding herself. Encourage her by giving her 'finger foods' to chew. Even toothless babies, who might hate lumpy food, usually enjoy holding and sucking or gnawing on chunks of food. Learning to chew finger foods early, even before teeth appear, can help prevent feeding problems later and give some relief to a baby whose teeth are just breaking through. Chewing on a piece of apple or toast is much more tasty (and nutritious) than a plastic teething ring! Toddlers and older children also like eating with their fingers, so there's no need to stop giving finger foods even when your child is proficient with a spoon.

Try to limit sugary foods, such as biscuits and bought rusks, because children can easily develop a sweet tooth which may lead to tooth decay later. Avoid small, hard, easy-to-swallow pieces of food, and remember never to give food to your baby while she is lying down, or to leave her alone when she is eating, because of the risk of choking.

Try some of the following ideas:

* Sticks or chunks of raw fruit and vegetables, such as carrot, apple, banana or celery. (Smaller babies with few teeth might find some of these – hard apple, carrot or celery, for example – too hard to manage.)

* Pieces of cheese

* Toasted bread, pitta bread, small savoury sandwiches, cooked pasta shapes (choose larger varieties like twists) or home-made rusks (see page 50)

Vegetable and Fruit Purées

Purées made from vegetables or fruit are ideal first foods for your baby.

Vegetable Purées Almost any vegetable can be cooked and puréed for your baby. Prepare vegetables by washing or peeling and removing any seeds or pips. Cut into pieces and steam or boil in a little water. Drain and purée in a blender or food processor, or rub through a sieve. Add a little water or milk (breast or formula milk for babies under six months), if necessary, to give a smooth, soft consistency. Most vegetable purées freeze well. Freeze in small portions (ice cube trays are useful) and thaw and reheat thoroughly as required. Use within one month.

Fruit Purées Choose ripe fruits. Prepare by removing skins, cores, pips or stones and cutting into small pieces. Some fruits, such as ripe pears, bananas, peaches and plums, need no cooking and can simply be sieved or puréed. Hard fruits, like apples, should be stewed in a little water or apple juice until soft and then puréed in a blender or food processor or rubbed through a sieve. Dried fruits, such as apricots or prunes, can also be used for making purées – look for additive-free varieties. Soak overnight in water, drain and cook in a little water or apple juice until soft, then purée. Freeze in small portions. (Banana is not suitable for freezing.) Use within one month and thaw thoroughly before giving to your baby.

Baby Muesli

Suitable from about 6 months

Keep the basic mixture in an airtight container and use as required.

> *2 oz (50 g) porridge oats*
> *1 tsp (5 ml) wheatgerm (optional)*
> *2 oz (50 g) wholewheat flakes*
> *1 tbsp (15 ml) skimmed milk powder*

Place all the ingredients in a blender or food processor and blend until the mixture resembles fine breadcrumbs. To serve, soak in milk or fruit juice and top with a little puréed fruit or mashed banana.

Banana Breakfast

Suitable from about 6 months

> *½ wholewheat breakfast biscuit (eg. Weetabix)*
> *a little milk (warm or cold)*
> *½ small banana*

Crumble the biscuit into a bowl and pour over enough milk to moisten. Peel and mash the banana well and mix into the cereal.

Lentil Purée

Suitable from about 5 months

> *2 oz (50 g) split red lentils, rinsed*
> *¼ pint (150 ml) water*

Put the lentils and water in a saucepan, bring to the boil, cover and simmer for about 20 minutes or until tender, adding a little more water if necessary. Purée in a blender or food processor, or rub through a sieve, until smooth.

Vegetable Broth

Suitable from 4–5 months

> *1 carrot, chopped*
> *1 small potato, chopped*
> *2 oz (50 g) fresh or frozen peas*
> *2 oz (50 g) frozen sweetcorn*
> *4 fl oz (100 ml) water*
> *4 fl oz (100 ml) milk (breast or formula milk for babies under six months)*

Put the vegetables and water in a saucepan. Bring to the boil, cover and simmer for about 20 minutes or until tender. Add the milk and purée in a blender or food processor, or rub through a sieve, until smooth.
* Can be frozen

Beef and Vegetable Casserole

Suitable from about 5 months

> 2 oz (50 g) lean beef, chopped
> 1 small potato, chopped
> 1 small carrot or small piece of swede, chopped
> 1 oz (25 g) fresh or frozen peas
> 1 tomato, skinned, seeded and chopped
> about 4 fl oz (100 ml) water

Put all the ingredients in a small saucepan, bring to the boil, cover and simmer for about 25 minutes or until the meat and vegetables are tender. Strain and reserve the cooking liquid. Purée the meat and vegetables in a blender or food processor until smooth, adding enough of the reserved liquid to give a soft consistency.

Liver and Tomato Casserole

Suitable from about 5 months

> 4 oz (100 g) lamb's liver, thinly sliced
> 1 small tomato, skinned, seeded and chopped
> 2 fl oz (50 ml) tomato juice
> 1 small potato, chopped

Put all the ingredients in a small saucepan, bring to the boil, cover and simmer for 15–20 minutes or until the liver and potato are tender. Purée in a blender or food processor until smooth.
* Can be frozen

Chicken Casserole

Suitable from about 5 months

> 2–3 oz (50–75 g) raw chicken meat, skinned and chopped
> 3–4 oz (75–100 g) prepared vegetables (eg. carrot, peas,
>   swede, potato)
> 4 fl oz (100 ml) water or Vegetable Stock (see page 64)

Put all the ingredients in a small saucepan, bring to the boil, cover and simmer for about 20 minutes or until the chicken is thoroughly cooked and the vegetables are tender. Strain and reserve the cooking liquid. Purée the chicken and vegetables in a blender or food processor, adding enough of the reserved liquid to give a soft consistency.
* Can be frozen

Egg and Vegetables

Suitable from about 6 months

> 1–2 tbsp (15–30 ml) milk
> 1 egg yolk
> 3–4 oz (75–100 g) cooked vegetables (eg. potato, carrot,
>   parsnip, peas, lentils or a mixture)

Beat together the milk and egg yolk and pour into a small non-stick saucepan. Cook for about 5 minutes or until thoroughly scrambled, stirring constantly. Turn into a blender or food processor, add the vegetables and purée until smooth.

Fish and Rice Savoury

Suitable from about 6 months

> 2–3 oz (50–75 g) cod or haddock fillet, cooked
> 2–3 tbsp (30–45 ml) cooked brown rice
> 1 tbsp (15 ml) cooked peas or sweetcorn
> 2 tbsp (30 ml) Greek-style natural yogurt

Flake the fish and combine with the rice and peas or sweetcorn. Stir in the yogurt and purée in a blender or food processor.

Fish in Cheese Sauce
Suitable from about 6 months

> *3 oz (75 g) white fish fillet, skinned*
> *2 fl oz (50 ml) milk*
> *1 oz (25 g) Cheddar cheese, grated*
> *1 tsp (5 ml) baby rice*

Put the fish in a saucepan, add the milk and poach gently for about 5 minutes or until the fish flakes easily. Flake the fish in the milk. Add the cheese and baby rice and stir until the cheese has melted. Turn into a blender or food processor and purée until smooth.

Cottage Cheese and Potato
Suitable from about 6 months

> *4 oz (100 g) potato, boiled and puréed (or a mixture of*
> *cooked puréed vegetables)*
> *1 oz (25 g) low-fat soft cheese or cottage cheese*

Mix together the potato and cheese, adding a little milk if necessary to make a soft purée.

Macaroni Cheese
Suitable from about 6 months

> *2–3 oz (50–75 g) cooked macaroni (or other small pasta)*
> *1 oz (25 g) Cheddar cheese, grated*
> *a little milk*

Put the macaroni and cheese in a blender or food processor and purée until smooth, adding a little milk to give a soft consistency.

Rice and Beans

Suitable from about 5 months

2 oz (50 g) cooked rice
*2 oz (50 g) cooked or canned beans (eg. red kidney, butter
  or haricot beans), drained*
2 oz (50 g) cooked vegetables (eg. carrot, peas or swede)
*a little water or milk (breast or formula milk for babies under
  six months)*

Put the rice and vegetables in a blender or food processor and
purée until smooth, adding enough water or milk to give a soft
consistency.

Vegetable Hotpot

Suitable from about 5 months

*4 oz (100 g) prepared vegetables (eg. potato, carrot, swede
  or peas)*
*2–3 oz (50–75 g) cooked beans (eg. red kidney, butter or
  haricot beans)*

Cook the vegetables in a little boiling water until tender. Drain,
reserving the liquid. Put the vegetables in a blender or food
processor with the beans and purée until smooth, adding a little
of the reserved cooking water to give a soft consistency.

Mixed Vegetable Purée

Suitable from about 4 months

4 oz (100 g) potato, chopped
4 oz (100 g) prepared fresh vegetables (eg. peas, beans,
*   cauliflower, carrot or swede), or frozen vegetables*
a little milk (breast or formula milk for babies under six
*   months)*

Cook the vegetables in a little boiling water until tender. Drain and purée in a blender or food processor until smooth, adding a little milk to give a soft consistency.
* Can be frozen

Peach and Yogurt Dessert

Suitable from about 6 months

1 medium peach, skinned, stoned and chopped
2–3 tbsp (30–45 ml) natural yogurt (Greek-style, low-fat or
*   whole milk yogurt)*

Purée the peach in a blender or food processor or rub through a sieve. Combine with the yogurt.

Apple and Apricot Purée

Suitable from about 4 months

Any combination of stewed fruits can be used for making this dessert. It can also be served as a topping for breakfast cereal or yogurt.

1 small eating apple, peeled, cored and chopped
2 oz (50 g) dried apricots, soaked overnight, drained
3–4 tbsp (45–60 ml) apple juice

Put the apple and apricots in a saucepan with the fruit juice and simmer gently for about 10 minutes or until soft. Turn into a blender or food processor and purée until smooth, or rub through a sieve. Serve warm or cold.
* Can be frozen

Apricot Rice Pudding

Suitable from about 4 months

Any dried fruit can be used for this dessert but make sure any seeds or stones are removed by sieving the cooked fruit before puréeing.

> *2 oz (50 g) dried apricots, soaked overnight, drained*
> *3–4 tbsp (45–60 ml) apple juice*
> *2 oz (50 g) cooked pudding rice*

Chop the apricots and put in a saucepan with the apple juice. Cook gently for a few minutes or until soft. Put in a blender or food processor with the rice and purée until smooth, adding a little more fruit juice if necessary.
* Can be frozen

Fruit and Cheese Dessert

Suitable from about 6 months

Any puréed fruit can be used to make this quick dessert. Some, such as ripe pear or peach, do not need cooking before being puréed.

> *2–3 oz (50–75 g) puréed fruit (eg. apple, apricot, plum, pear*
> *or peach) or ½ medium banana, mashed*
> *2 oz (50 g) low-fat soft cheese (salt-free if possible)*

Mix together the puréed fruit and cheese, stirring until well blended.

BETTER BREAKFASTS

Although there is no evidence to show that children who skip breakfast are less able to concentrate at school, it is still worth encouraging your child to eat a healthy breakfast. Children have high energy and nutrient requirements and a decent breakfast will ensure your child gets a good proportion of what her body needs. It may also help prevent her feeling hungry at break-time and filling up with crisps, sweets, biscuits and fizzy drinks from the tuck shop.

Cereal, milk and toast are popular and healthy choices for breakfast. Add some fresh fruit or fruit juice and your child will be getting a really nourishing start to the day. All the following recipes can be made very quickly and will make a satisfying and nutritious change from cereal and toast.

To make breakfast as healthy as possible, simply follow the better breakfast guide (see opposite).

Muesli

Quick and simple to make, this muesli can be stored in an airtight container and used as required. Top with Dried Fruit Salad (page 130) or fresh fruit, if liked.

Makes about 12 oz (350 g)

> *4 oz (100 g) rolled oats*
> *4 oz (100 g) whole wheat or bran flakes*
> *2 oz (50 g) nuts, chopped and toasted*
> *2 oz (50 g) seedless raisins or chopped no-soak dried apricots*
> *1 oz (25 g) soft brown sugar (optional)*

Combine all the ingredients and store in an airtight container. Serve with milk, fruit juice or natural yogurt.

Better breakfast guide

Cut down on these

* highly refined, sugar-coated cereals. (Some have over 50 per cent sugar and are low in fibre. Ignore claims about added vitamins on these products – vitamins are usually added to replace losses during processing.)

* butter, lard, blended oils, block margarine

* sugary spreads, such as jam, marmalade and honey

* squashes and fruit drinks. (Fruit *juice drinks* and fruit *flavoured drinks* can contain as little as 10 per cent fruit juice; fruit *flavour* drinks may contain no juice at all.)

* bacon and processed meats, such as black pudding and sausages

Choose more of these

* unrefined breakfast cereals with little or no added sugar (such as porridge, Shredded Wheat, Weetabix and sugar-free muesli). Some, like Weetabix and Ready Brek, are suitable for babies of about six to seven months, and are much cheaper than baby breakfast cereals.

* polyunsaturated margarine and oil for spreading and cooking

* pure fruit spreads and savoury spreads (such as yeast extract and peanut butter)

* pure fruit juice – best diluted for children

* wholemeal bread. (All bread is nutritious but the higher fibre content of wholemeal bread makes it the healthiest choice.)

* semi-skimmed or skimmed milk when your child is old enough (see page 11)

Fruity Porridge
Serves 4

> *2 oz (50 g) no-soak dried apricots, chopped*
> *1 medium eating apple, peeled, cored and chopped*
> *2 tsp (10 ml) sugar or honey (optional)*
> *1 pint (568 ml) milk (whole, semi-skimmed or skimmed) or*
> *water*
> *3 oz (75 g) porridge oats*

Mix together the apricots, apple and sugar or honey, if using. Pour the milk or water into a saucepan and sprinkle on the porridge oats. Bring to the boil, stirring, and cook for 1 minute. Add the fruit mixture and simmer, stirring, for about 3 minutes or until the porridge is thick. Serve hot.

Fruity Yogurt Pots
Serves 4

> *1 eating apple, cored and chopped*
> *1 medium banana, sliced*
> *1 peach, stoned and chopped or 4 oz (100 g) peaches*
> *canned in fruit juice, drained and chopped*
> *4 oz (100 g) seedless grapes, halved*
> *4 oz (100 g) raspberries, thawed if frozen*
> *12 fl oz (350 ml) Greek-style natural yogurt*
> *4 tsp (20 ml) clear honey (optional)*

Mix together all the fruits and stir in the yogurt. Divide between small pots or dishes and top with a little honey, if liked.

Cheese and Tomato Toasts

This simple recipe is ideal for breakfast or a quick snack.

Serves 4

> *4 small tomatoes, sliced*
> *4 slices of wholemeal bread, toasted*
> *4 oz (100 g) Cheddar cheese, sliced*
> *½ tsp (2.5 ml) dried oregano or mixed herbs (optional)*

Place a layer of tomato slices on each piece of toast and grill under a moderate heat for 1–2 minutes or until the tomatoes begin to soften. Cover with slices of cheese and sprinkle with herbs, if liked. Grill until the cheese is bubbling and golden, then serve immediately.

Tomato and Cheese Scramble

Serves 2

> *2 eggs, beaten*
> *2 tbsp (30 ml) milk*
> *½ oz (15 g) polyunsaturated margarine*
> *½ oz (15 g) Cheddar cheese, grated*
> *1–2 medium tomatoes, chopped*
> *2 slices of wholemeal toast, to serve*

Beat together the eggs and milk. Melt the margarine in a saucepan, pour in the egg mixture and cook over a gentle heat, stirring continuously, until the eggs become thick and lumpy and are thoroughly cooked. Remove from the heat and stir in the cheese and tomatoes. Serve immediately on wholemeal toast.

SOUPS, DIPS AND SPREADS

Warming soups make an ideal meal for children of all ages. Served with wholemeal bread, they provide a good range of nutrients – puréed soups are an easy way of disguising vegetables, too. Thicker soups are easier for young children to eat because they stay on the spoon. Liven them up by sprinkling a few tiny cubes of toasted bread on top, or stamp out tiny shapes from toast with petit four cutters and float them on top of the soup.

Dips are an ideal way of getting children to eat raw vegetables, especially if they are allowed to help themselves. Packed into small pots and accompanied by some vegetable sticks or bread, they are good food for picnics and lunchboxes, too. Any of the dips in the following recipe section can also be used for spreading on toast or in sandwiches.

Vegetable Stock

This stock is quick and simple to make and, unlike stock cubes, contains no salt or additives (such as monosodium glutamate). Add any vegetables you happen to have, such as chopped onion, carrot, leek, celery or mushrooms, to add flavour. If you do add vegetables, simmer the stock for at least 1 hour before straining. Omit pepper for very young babies.

Makes 1 pint (600 ml)

> *1 pint (600 ml) water*
> *1 bouquet garni*
> *freshly ground pepper*

Place the water in a saucepan, bring to the boil and add the bouquet garni. Simmer for 10 minutes, remove the bouquet garni and season with pepper to taste.

Vegetable Soup

Serves 6

4 celery sticks, chopped
4 oz (100 g) cabbage, shredded
8 oz (225 g) courgettes, sliced
8 oz (225 g) potatoes, chopped
4 oz (100 g) fresh or frozen peas
2 oz (50 g) mushrooms, sliced
½ pint (300 ml) tomato juice
1 pint (600 ml) Vegetable Stock (page 64)
2 tsp (10 ml) chopped fresh or 1 tsp (5 ml) dried parsley
freshly ground pepper

Place all the ingredients, except the pepper, in a large saucepan, bring to the boil, cover and simmer for about 40 minutes or until all the vegetables are tender. Season to taste with pepper.

Sweetcorn Chowder

Serves 4–6

2 oz (50 g) lean bacon rashers
2 tsp (10 ml) polyunsaturated oil
1 medium onion, chopped
1 lb (450 g) potatoes, cut into bite-sized chunks
10 oz (275 g) frozen sweetcorn
1½ pints (900 ml) Vegetable Stock (page 64)
freshly ground pepper
½ pint (300 ml) milk (whole, semi-skimmed or skimmed)

Remove the rind from the bacon and cut into strips. Heat the oil in a saucepan, add the bacon and onion and fry gently for about 5 minutes or until the onion is soft. Add the potatoes, sweetcorn, stock and a little pepper. Bring to the boil and simmer for 25–30 minutes or until the potatoes are tender. Add the milk and reheat before serving.

Leek and Potato Soup

Serves 4–6

> 1 lb (450 g) leeks, trimmed and sliced
> 2 medium potatoes, cubed
> 1 tbsp (15 ml) polyunsaturated margarine
> 1 pint (600 ml) Vegetable Stock (page 64) or water
> ½ pint (300 ml) milk (whole, semi-skimmed or skimmed)
> freshly ground pepper (optional)

Place the leeks, potatoes, margarine and a few spoonfuls of stock or water in a large saucepan. Stir well, bring to the boil, cover and simmer for about 20 minutes. Add the remaining stock or water and cook for a further 10 minutes or until the vegetables are tender. Remove from the heat, add the milk and purée in a blender or food processor until smooth. Season with pepper, if liked, and reheat gently before serving.

Bean and Potato Soup

Serves 6–8

> 2 pints (1.2 litres) Vegetable Stock (page 64)
> 8 oz (225 g) potatoes, chopped
> 8 oz (225 g) onions, chopped
> 8 oz (225 g) cooked red kidney beans
> freshly ground black pepper

Put the stock, potatoes and onions in a large saucepan, bring to the boil, cover and simmer for 10–15 minutes or until the potatoes are tender. Remove from the heat, add the beans and purée in a blender or food processor until smooth. Season to taste with black pepper and reheat before serving.

Lentil Soup
Serves 4–6

3 oz (75 g) split red lentils, rinsed
1½ pints (900 ml) Vegetable Stock (page 64) or water
8 oz (225 g) canned chopped tomatoes
1 small onion, chopped
8 oz (225 g) potatoes, chopped
freshly ground pepper

Put the lentils in a large saucepan with the stock or water, tomatoes and onion. Bring to the boil, cover and simmer for about 35 minutes or until the lentils are soft. Add the potato and cook for a further 15–20 minutes or until tender. Cool slightly, then purée in a blender or food processor, or rub through a sieve. Return to the pan, season with pepper and reheat before serving.

Hummus
Makes about 10 oz (275 g)

4 oz (100 g) dried chick peas, soaked overnight, or one 14 oz
*   (400 g) can chick peas*
juice of 1 lemon
2 tbsp (30 ml) tahini (sesame seed paste)
1 tbsp (15 ml) olive oil or polyunsaturated oil
small garlic clove (optional)
freshly ground pepper
wholemeal pitta bread, toast fingers or vegetable sticks, to
*   serve*

If using dried chick peas, drain and place them in a saucepan. Cover with fresh water, bring to the boil, then cover and simmer for about 1 hour or until tender.

Drain the chick peas and place them in a blender or food processor with the lemon juice. Blend to a smooth purée, adding a little extra water if the mixture is too thick. Add the tahini, oil, garlic, if using, and a little pepper and blend again until smooth. Transfer to a serving dish and serve with the pitta bread, toast fingers or vegetable sticks.

Cottage Cheese Dip

Serves 3–4

> 8 oz (225 g) tub cottage cheese (plain or with chives)
> 2–3 tbsp (30–45 ml) milk
> 1 small onion, finely chopped
> freshly ground pepper
> wholemeal pitta bread, toast fingers or vegetable sticks, to
> serve

Sieve the cottage cheese with the milk or purée in a blender or food processor. Turn into a bowl and mix in the onion. Season to taste with pepper. Transfer to a serving dish and serve with the pitta bread, toast fingers or vegetable sticks.

Butter Bean Dip

Makes about 10 oz (275 g)

> one 14 oz (400 g) can butter beans, drained and rinsed
> 1 tbsp (15 ml) olive oil or polyunsaturated oil
> 1–2 tbsp (15–30 ml) lemon juice
> 1 tsp (5 ml) chopped fresh or ½ tsp (2.5 ml) dried parsley
> 2 tsp (10 ml) tomato purée
> wholemeal pitta bread, toast fingers or vegetable sticks, to
> serve

Put all the ingredients in a blender or food processor and purée until smooth. Transfer to a serving dish and serve with the pitta bread, toast fingers or vegetable sticks.

Sardine Dip

This creamy dip can also be used as a spread for toast or sandwiches.

Serves 6

> 4 oz (100 g) can sardines in tomato sauce
> 8 oz (225 g) curd cheese
> 1 tbsp (15 ml) lemon juice
> sticks of raw carrot, cucumber (or other crunchy vegetables),
> toast, wholemeal pitta bread or grissini (bread sticks), to
> serve

Remove any bones from the sardines and mash until smooth. Add the remaining ingredients and mix well. Transfer to a small serving bowl and serve with the vegetable sticks, toast, pitta bread or *grissini*.

Lentil and Mushroom Pâté

This pâté is delicious served with warm wholemeal pitta bread or crusty bread and ideal for filling rolls or sandwiches for a packed lunch.

Serves 4

> *4 oz (100 g) brown lentils, rinsed*
> *½ pint (300 ml) water*
> *3 tbsp (45 ml) polyunsaturated oil*
> *3 oz (75 g) mushrooms, finely chopped*
> *1 garlic clove (optional)*
> *1 tbsp (15 ml) tahini (sesame seed paste) or peanut butter*
> *2 tsp (10 ml) chopped fresh or 1 tsp (5 ml) dried parsley*
> *2 tbsp (30 ml) lemon juice*
> *freshly ground pepper*

Put the lentils in a saucepan with the water, bring to the boil, cover and simmer for about 30 minutes or until tender, then drain and mash. Heat the oil in a saucepan and fry the mushrooms and garlic, if using, for 2–3 minutes or until soft. Add the lentils, tahini, parsley and lemon juice and cook for a further minute, stirring constantly. Season to taste with pepper. Transfer to a serving dish and chill until required.

Fruit Dip

Use any fresh or stewed fruit purée as the basis for a sweet dip.

Mix together equal quantities of mashed or puréed fruit and low-fat soft cheese or Greek-style natural yogurt. Serve with slices or chunks of fresh fruit, such as apples, pineapple or pears.

Sugar-free Jam

This fruity jam is made without adding the large quantity of sugar found in bought jam. It can be kept, chilled, for up to a week.

Makes about 12 oz (350 g)

> *8 oz (225 g) prepared fresh fruits (eg. strawberries,*
> *raspberries, blackcurrants, apricots or plums)*
> *2 fl oz (50 ml) concentrated apple juice*
> *2 oz (50 g) arrowroot*

Put the fruit and apple juice in a saucepan and cook gently until soft. Dissolve the arrowroot in 2 tbsp (30 ml) water and add to the fruit mixture, stirring continuously. Simmer, stirring frequently, for a further 15 minutes or until the jam is thick. Pour into a clean jar, cover and refrigerate.

Apricot and Raisin Spread

This fruity spread contains more nutrients than ordinary jam, but the natural sugar can still cause tooth decay.

Makes about 4 oz (100 g)

> *6 oz (175 g) no-soak dried apricots, chopped*
> *1 oz (25 g) sultanas or seedless raisins*
> *¼ pint (150 ml) water*

Put the fruit in a saucepan with the water. Bring to the boil, then simmer until soft. Drain off the liquid and reserve. Purée the fruit in a blender or food processor, adding enough of the reserved liquid to make a smooth purée. Spread on bread or toast.

SUPER SALADS

There's more to salads than limp lettuce. Even if your child usually refuses to try salads, the interesting colours and textures of the recipes in this section are almost certain to tempt her. Wash salad vegetables really well in cold running water. If you're using organic vegetables, the skins can be left on things like cucumber, but non-organic produce is best peeled.

Vinaigrette

Makes about 4 tbsp (60 ml)

> *3 tbsp (45 ml) olive oil or polyunsaturated oil*
> *1 tbsp (15 ml) wine vinegar or lemon juice*
> *¼ tsp (1.25 ml) sugar*
> *¼ tsp (1.25 ml) mustard powder*
> *salt and freshly ground pepper (optional)*

Put all the ingredients in a small screw-topped jar, adding salt and pepper to taste, if liked. Shake until well blended. Alternatively, put the ingredients in a small bowl and whisk until well blended.

Simple Salad

Serves 4

> ½ small Chinese cabbage, shredded
> 3 oz (75 g) bean sprouts
> 1 oz (25 g) button mushrooms, sliced
> small bunch of watercress, trimmed and separated into
>   sprigs
> 4 tbsp (60 ml) Vinaigrette (page 71)

Put the cabbage, bean sprouts, mushrooms and watercress in a large salad bowl. Pour over the vinaigrette and toss well just before serving.

Salad Gardens

These miniature salads are an ideal way to tempt toddlers to eat fresh vegetables.

Makes 8

> 1 small carrot, grated
> 2 inch (5 cm) piece of cucumber, chopped
> ¼ punnet salad cress
> 2 oz (50 g) Edam cheese
> 8 cherry tomatoes

Put a little carrot and cucumber in the bottom of each of eight paper bun cases and top with a little cress. Cut the cheese into ¼ inch (0.5 cm) thick slices and cut out small shapes with a sharp knife or with petit four cutters. Top each salad with one or two cheese shapes and a cherry tomato.

Salad Kebabs

Kebabs are a good way of combining different foods, and they appeal to children because they can be eaten with the fingers. Stick to bite-sized chunks of foods that your child likes, or add something new to try. **Kebab sticks and skewers are not suitable for young children – use plastic drinking straws as an alternative.**

Makes 5

   5 low-fat chipolata sausages or Vegebangers, grilled and
     cooled
   3 inch (7.5 cm) piece of cucumber
   1 small green pepper
   3 oz (75 g) Edam cheese
   10 seedless grapes
   5 button mushrooms
   10 cherry tomatoes

TO SERVE
shredded lettuce
5 small wholemeal pitta breads, warmed

Cut the sausages in half. Peel the cucumber, cut into ½ inch
(1 cm) slices and cut each slice across in half. Core and seed the
green pepper and cut into pieces. Cut the cheese into bite-sized
cubes. Divide the ingredients between five straws, piercing with
a skewer first if necessary. Serve on a bed of shredded lettuce
with warm pitta breads.

Three Bean Salad

This salad is ideal for busy parents as the beans used all come
from cans!

Serves 6–8

   14 oz (400 g) can red kidney beans
   14 oz (400 g) can chick peas
   14 oz (400 g) can flageolet beans
   2 tbsp (30 ml) polyunsaturated oil or olive oil
   1 tbsp (15 ml) lemon juice
   freshly ground pepper
   chopped fresh parsley, to garnish (optional)

Drain and rinse the beans in cold water. Whisk together the olive
oil and lemon juice and season to taste with pepper. Toss the
beans in the dressing, transfer to a serving bowl and sprinkle
with parsley, if liked.

Fruity Pasta Salad

Serves 3–4

> 2 oz (50 g) wholewheat pasta bows, twists or other shapes
> 1 oz (25 g) fresh or frozen peas, cooked
> 1 small carrot, chopped
> 1 oz (25 g) seedless grapes, halved
> 1 small orange or 2 small tangerines
> 2 oz (50 g) Cheddar cheese

Cook the pasta in boiling water for about 12 minutes or according to the directions on the packet. Drain, cool and put in a salad bowl. Add the peas, carrot and grapes to the pasta. Peel the orange and cut into bite-sized pieces. (If using tangerines, peel and break into segments.) Add to the pasta mixture. Slice the cheese thickly and either cut into cubes or stamp out shapes with petit four cutters. Sprinkle on top of the salad and serve.

Chicken and Apple Salad

Serves 3–4

> 8 oz (225 g) boiled potatoes, cubed
> 8 oz (225 g) cooked chicken meat, chopped
> 1 large eating apple, cored and sliced
> 2 oz (50 g) cooked fresh or frozen peas
> 1 tbsp (15 ml) mayonnaise
> 2 tbsp (30 ml) Greek-style or low-fat natural yogurt

Put the potatoes, chicken, apple and peas in a salad bowl. Mix together the mayonnaise and yogurt, add to the other ingredients and toss well.

Carrot and Raisin Salad

Serves 2–3

> 4 large carrots, grated
> 3 oz (75 g) seedless raisins or sultanas
> 3–4 tbsp (45–60 ml) orange juice or Vinaigrette (page 71)
> 1 tbsp (15 ml) sunflower or sesame seeds, toasted (optional)

74

Put the carrots and raisins or sultanas in a serving bowl and pour over the orange juice or vinaigrette. Toss well and sprinkle with sunflower or sesame seeds, if liked.

Apple and Celery Salad

This is an ideal salad to serve during the winter months, when salad ingredients tend to be expensive. Red-skinned apples add extra colour.

Serves 2–3

> *2 large red eating apples, cored and chopped*
> *a little lemon juice*
> *½ small head of celery, chopped*
> *1 oz (25 g) finely chopped walnuts or toasted sunflower*
>   *seeds*
> *2 oz (50 g) stoned dates, chopped*
> *2 tbsp (30 ml) mayonnaise or Vinaigrette (page 71)*

Toss the apples in a little lemon juice and put in a salad bowl with the celery, walnuts or sunflower seeds and dates. Add the mayonnaise or vinaigrette, and toss until all the ingredients are well coated.

Fruity Coleslaw Salad

Serves 4

> *8 oz (225 g) white or red cabbage, finely shredded*
> *2 medium carrots, grated*
> *1 eating apple, peeled, cored and grated*
> *1 oz (25 g) seedless raisins*
> *½ oz (15 g) sunflower seeds*
> *1 tbsp (15 ml) mayonnaise*
> *2 tbsp (30 ml) Greek-style or low-fat natural yogurt*
> *1 tsp (5 ml) lemon juice*

Put the cabbage, carrot, apple, raisins and sunflower seeds in a serving bowl. Mix together the mayonnaise, yogurt and lemon juice and stir into the cabbage mixture. Toss well before serving.

Whole Wheat Salad

Serves 3–4

4 oz (100 g) whole wheat grain
1 large carrot, coarsely grated
1 small apple, cored and chopped
4 inch (10 cm) piece of cucumber, chopped
1 oz (25 g) seedless raisins or sultanas
1 tbsp (15 ml) mayonnaise mixed with 2 tbsp (30 ml) natural
*   yogurt, or 3 tbsp (45 ml) Vinaigrette (page 71)*

Soak the wheat overnight in cold water. Drain and place in a saucepan with plenty of boiling water. Simmer for about 25 minutes or until tender. Drain and rinse in cold water.

Put the cooked whole wheat in a salad bowl with the carrot, apple, cucumber and raisins or sultanas. Add the mayonnaise mixture or vinaigrette and toss until all the salad ingredients are well coated.

Yogurt and Cucumber Salad

Serve this cooling salad with vegetable sticks, warm pitta bread or toast fingers.

Serves 2–3

½ cucumber
¼ pint (150 ml) Greek-style natural yogurt
1 garlic clove, crushed or finely chopped (optional)
1 tbsp (15 ml) chopped fresh mint
1 tsp (5 ml) lemon juice
freshly ground pepper
mint sprigs, to garnish (optional)

Scrub the cucumber and chop finely. Pat off the excess moisture with absorbent kitchen paper. Mix all the ingredients together in a serving bowl, adding freshly ground pepper to taste. Chill in the refrigerator until required. Garnish with a few mint sprigs before serving, if liked.

Potato Salad

Serves 4

1 lb (450 g) new potatoes or waxy old potatoes
2 oz (50 g) onion, finely chopped
1 tsp (5 ml) chopped fresh or dried parsley (optional)
1 tbsp (15 ml) mayonnaise
2 tbsp (30 ml) Greek-style or low-fat natural yogurt

Cook the potatoes in boiling water until tender. Drain and cut into bite-sized pieces. Leave to cool.

Mix together the onion, parsley (if using), mayonnaise and yogurt, then stir gently into the potatoes until evenly coated. Chill until required.

Pasta and Tuna Salad

This salad is ideal for storing in small pots ready to be used in a packed lunch or for a picnic. It also makes a delicious filling for pitta bread.

Serves 2–3

2 oz (50 g) wholewheat pasta shapes
3 oz (75 g) canned tuna fish in natural juices, drained and
    flaked
1 tomato, chopped
3 tbsp (45 ml) Greek-style natural yogurt or mayonnaise
cucumber slices, to garnish

Cook the pasta in boiling water for about 12 minutes or according to the directions on the packet. Drain and leave to cool. Put the pasta in a bowl and stir in the tuna, tomato and yogurt or mayonnaise. Garnish with a few cucumber slices before serving.

FISH

Fish is an excellent food for growing children. Although there is no truth in the rumour that fish is especially good for children's brains, it *is* a good source of protein, vitamins and minerals. Cheaper fish are just as nutritious as more expensive varieties, and cooking fish from scratch is far cheaper than buying ready-made dishes. Buy fish from a shop with a regular turnover and check that there are no bones remaining before giving it to your child. If your child's idea of fish is fish fingers, then why not try the home-made version on page 102 – they are better value and contain more fish than those in the shops – *and* they are completely free of additives.

Kedgeree

Use white fish for this version of kedgeree as smoked fish is usually salty and may also contain artificial colourings.

Serves 3–4

> *8 oz (225 g) haddock or cod fillet, skinned*
> *1 oz (25 g) polyunsaturated margarine*
> *8 oz (225 g) cooked long grain brown rice*
> *3 oz (75 g) fresh or frozen peas or sweetcorn, cooked*
>   *(optional)*
> *2 hard-boiled eggs, chopped*

Grill or steam the fish until thoroughly cooked, then flake finely. Melt the margarine in a saucepan. Add the fish, rice and peas or sweetcorn, if using, and stir until thoroughly heated. Remove from the heat and stir in the chopped egg. Serve immediately.

Pilchard Savoury

Serves 2–4

7 oz (200 g) canned pilchards in tomato sauce
1 lb (450 g) potatoes, boiled and mashed with a little milk
   and polyunsaturated margarine
2 oz (50 g) Cheddar cheese, grated
tomato slices, to garnish

Mash the pilchards and place in the bottom of an ovenproof
dish. Cover with a layer of mashed potatoes, sprinkle with grated
cheese and bake in the oven at 180°C (350°F) mark 4 for 25–30
minutes or until golden brown. Garnish with tomato slices before
serving.

Fishcakes

Even reluctant fish eaters are sure to enjoy these mild-flavoured
fishcakes.

Makes 8

8 oz (225 g) white fish fillet (eg. cod or haddock), skinned
8 oz (225 g) potato, boiled and mashed
1 tsp (5 ml) lemon juice
2 tsp (10 ml) tomato purée
2 tsp (10 ml) chopped fresh parsley
freshly ground pepper
1 egg, beaten
3 oz (75 g) wholemeal breadcrumbs

Grill or steam the fish until thoroughly cooked, then flake finely.
Mix together the potato, fish, lemon juice, tomato purée and
parsley and add pepper to taste. Bind with a little of the beaten
egg. Divide the mixture into eight portions and, using floured
hands, shape into cakes. Brush each fishcake with beaten egg
and coat with breadcrumbs. Cook the fishcakes under a moderate grill for about 10 minutes, turning once. Serve warm.

Simple Fisherman's Pie

Serves 3–4

> *10 oz (275 g) cod or haddock steak*
> *2–3 oz (50–75 g) frozen mixed vegetables, peas or*
>   *sweetcorn, cooked*
> *4 fl oz (100 ml) milk or fish stock*
> *10 oz (275 g) cooked potatoes, mashed with a little milk and*
>   *polyunsaturated margarine*
> *2 oz (50 g) Cheddar cheese, grated (optional)*

Grill, steam or poach the fish until thoroughly cooked, then flake finely. If poaching the fish, reserve the stock. Place the fish and vegetables in a 1 pint (600 ml) ovenproof dish. Pour over the milk or fish stock and cover with mashed potato. Sprinkle over the grated cheese, if using. Bake in the oven at 180°C (350°F) mark 4 for 30 minutes.

Cod and Tomato Parcels

Serves 4

> *4 cod fillets or portions, each weighing about 4 oz (100 g)*
> *1 tbsp (15 ml) polyunsaturated oil*
> *1 medium onion, chopped*
> *15 oz (425 g) can of chopped tomatoes*
> *1 tbsp (15 ml) tomato purée*
> *2 oz (50 g) mushrooms, sliced (optional)*
> *chopped fresh parsley, to garnish*

Cut our four 10 inch (25 cm) squares of kitchen foil. Place one piece of fish in the centre of each. Heat the oil in a small saucepan and fry the onion for about 5 minutes or until soft. Add the chopped tomatoes and tomato purée and cook for a further 5 minutes. Spoon some of the sauce over each piece of cod and top with mushrooms, if liked. Wrap up each parcel, leaving a small hole in the top for steam to escape. Place on a baking sheet and bake in the oven at 190°C (375°F) mark 5 for 25–30 minutes. Transfer the fish and sauce to plates, sprinkle with chopped parsley and serve.

Fish Bites

Serves 3–4

> *3 oz (75 g) canned sardines in tomato sauce*
> *4 thick slices of wholemeal bread*
> *polyunsaturated margarine, for spreading*
> *tomato or cucumber slices (optional)*

Remove any bones from the sardines and mash until smooth. Toast the bread and spread with a little margarine. Spread some of the mashed sardines on each slice and cook under a moderate grill for about 1 minute. Cut into fingers, squares, triangles or other shapes and top each with a slice of tomato or cucumber, if liked.

Fun food

Use a fish-shaped cutter to stamp out shapes from the toast. Top each fish with a little of the sardine mixture and grill as above. Use a small piece of raw carrot or tomato to make an 'eye' for each fish. Serve on a 'sea' of shredded lettuce, watercress or salad cress.

Fish Savoury

Serves 1–2

> *3–4 oz (75–100 g) cod or haddock fillet, skinned*
> *1 hard-boiled egg*
> *3 tbsp (45 ml) milk*
> *2 tbsp (30 ml) wholemeal breadcrumbs*
> *½ oz (15 g) polyunsaturated margarine*

Grill or steam the fish until thoroughly cooked, then flake finely or mash. Shell and mash the egg and combine with the fish and milk. Place the mixture in a small ovenproof dish, top with breadcrumbs and dot with margarine. Bake in the oven at 190°C (375°F) mark 5 for 15 minutes.

Variation

Cheesy Topping Sprinkle ½–1 oz (15–25 g) grated Cheddar cheese over the breadcrumbs and bake as above until bubbling and golden.

FAMILY SUPPERS AND LUNCHES

Once your child reaches her first birthday she will probably be eating with the rest of the family. The recipes in this section are based on healthy ingredients and make nutritious main meals for the whole family. For younger babies (between six and 12 months), remove a small portion and either purée mash or chop.

Giving older children packed lunches to eat at school is one way to ensure they get something decent to eat during the day. The trouble with a lot of foods that traditionally end up in a lunchbox (pork pies, biscuits, crisps and processed meats, for instance) is that they are high in fat, sugar and salt and low in fibre. It is much better to use more healthy and nourishing alternatives, such as those suggested here.

Baked Chicken Risotto

Serves 4–6

> 2 tbsp (30 ml) polyunsaturated oil
> 1 lb (450 g) chicken meat, skinned and chopped
> 4 oz (100 g) onion, chopped
> 4 oz (100 g) carrot, chopped
> 4 oz (100 g) peas, thawed if frozen
> 4 oz (100 g) frozen sweetcorn, thawed
> 4 oz (100 g) long grain brown rice
> 1 pint (600 ml) Vegetable Stock (page 64)
> 1 tsp (5 ml) dried oregano or mixed herbs

Heat the oil in a saucepan, add the chicken, onion, carrot, peas, sweetcorn and rice and cook for 5 minutes, stirring occasionally, to seal in the juices. Transfer to a shallow ovenproof casserole. Pour over the stock and stir in the herbs. Cover and bake in the oven at 180°C (350°F) mark 4 for about 1 hour or until the meat is tender and the stock has been absorbed by the rice.

Chicken and Vegetables

Serves 4

1 tbsp (15 ml) polyunsaturated oil
1 small onion, chopped
1 lb (450 g) chicken meat, skinned and cut into cubes
7 fl oz (200 ml) Vegetable Stock (page 64)
4 oz (100 g) carrots, chopped
4 oz (100 g) fresh or frozen peas
4 oz (100 g) frozen or drained canned sweetcorn
6 oz (175 g) cooked red kidney or butter beans

Heat the oil in a large saucepan, add the chopped onion and cook for about 5 minutes or until soft. Add the chicken and cook for about 2 minutes or until browned. Add the stock and carrots, bring to the boil, then cover and simmer for about 45 minutes. Add the peas and sweetcorn and simmer for another 15 minutes or until the vegetables and chicken are tender. Add the cooked beans a few minutes before the end of cooking.

Chicken Hash

Serves 2–3

1 tbsp (15 ml) polyunsaturated oil
1 onion, finely chopped
1 large potato, grated
6 oz (175 g) cooked chicken meat, skinned and chopped
2 tbsp (30 ml) Vegetable Stock (page 64) or water
8 oz (225 g) baked beans
4 oz (100 g) fresh or frozen peas, cooked
2 tsp (10 ml) tomato purée
freshly ground pepper (optional)

Heat the oil in a saucepan, add the onion and potato and fry gently for about 10 minutes or until soft. Add the remaining ingredients and season with pepper, if liked. Cover and cook for a further 10 minutes, stirring occasionally to prevent sticking.

Chicken and Sweetcorn Bake

If your child dislikes cheese, simply leave the cheese out of the sauce.

Serves 4

> *8 oz (225 g) cooked chicken meat, skinned and diced or finely chopped*
> *4 oz (100 g) frozen sweetcorn, cooked*
> *½ pint (300 ml) Cheese Sauce (page 110)*
> *1 tsp (5 ml) chopped fresh parsley (optional)*
> *8 oz (225 g) potato, boiled*

Mix together the chicken and sweetcorn and stir into the sauce with the parsley, if using. Pour the mixture into a 1 pint (600 ml) ovenproof dish. Thinly slice the potatoes and arrange on top of the chicken mixture. Bake in the oven at 180°C (350°F) mark 4 for about 40 minutes or until the potatoes are just beginning to brown.

Beef Hotpot

Serve this economical, warming winter casserole with mashed potatoes or slices of wholemeal bread.

Serves 4–6

> *2 tbsp (30 ml) polyunsaturated oil*
> *1 large onion, chopped*
> *8 oz (225 g) carrots, sliced*
> *4 oz (100 g) swede or turnip, cubed*
> *12 oz (350 g) lean beef, cubed*
> *1 tbsp (15 ml) plain wholemeal flour*
> *1 tbsp (15 ml) tomato purée*
> *½ tsp (2.5 ml) dried mixed herbs (optional)*
> *about 1 pint (600 ml) Vegetable Stock (page 64)*
> *freshly ground pepper*
> *8 oz (225 g) cooked or canned beans (eg. red kidney or butter beans), drained*

Heat 1 tbsp (15 ml) of the oil in a flameproof casserole and fry the onion for about 5 minutes or until soft. Add the carrots and swede or turnip and cook for a few minutes, stirring occasionally. Remove the vegetables from the casserole and set aside.

Toss the meat in the flour. Heat the remaining oil in the casserole and fry the meat for 5 minutes or until browned on all sides. Add the vegetables and any remaining flour and stir well. Add the tomato purée and herbs, if using, then pour over enough stock just to cover the meat and vegetables. Season to taste with pepper. Bring to the boil, stirring occasionally, then cover and cook in the oven at 180°C (350°F) mark 4 for 1½–2 hours or until the meat and vegetables are tender. Add the beans and cook for a further 10 minutes.

Beef and Lentil Bake

Serves 4–6

8 oz (225 g) lean minced beef
1 medium onion, chopped
1 tsp (5 ml) dried mixed herbs
8 oz (225 g) cooked brown or green lentils
1 oz (25 g) plain wholemeal flour
¼ pint (150 ml) Vegetable Stock (page 64)
1 lb (450 g) potatoes, boiled and mashed with a little milk
    and polyunsaturated margarine
2 oz (50 g) Cheddar cheese, grated
tomato slices, to garnish

Put the mince in a saucepan and cook over a low heat for about 7 minutes or until brown, stirring occasionally. Drain off any excess fat. Add the onion and herbs and cook for a further 10 minutes or until the onion is soft. Stir in the cooked lentils. Sprinkle on the flour, mix well and cook for 1 minute, stirring continuously. Pour in the stock and mix well.

Turn the meat mixture into an ovenproof dish, top with the mashed potato and finish with a layer of grated cheese. Bake in the oven at 200°C (400°F) mark 6 for 25–30 minutes or until golden brown. Garnish with tomato slices before serving.

Beef and Potato Layer

Serves 4–6

> 1½ lb (700 g) potatoes
> 1–2 tbsp (15–30 ml) polyunsaturated oil
> 1 small onion, chopped
> 1 lb (450 g) lean minced beef
> 3 tbsp (45 ml) tomato purée
> 1 tsp (5 ml) dried mixed herbs
> ¼ pint (150 ml) Vegetable Stock (page 64)

Slice the potatoes thinly. Heat the oil in a saucepan and fry the onion for 2–3 minutes or until beginning to soften. Add the beef and fry for about 5 minutes or until browned. Add the remaining ingredients and cook for a further 2 minutes.

Put one-third of the potato slices into an oiled deep ovenproof dish and cover with half the meat mixture. Add another layer of potatoes and the remaining meat and cover with a final layer of potatoes. Cook in the oven at 180°C (350°F) mark 4 for about 1 hour or until the potatoes are soft and the top golden brown.

Oaty Meat Loaf

This substantial meat loaf can be served plain or with Tomato Sauce (page 90). It is delicious hot or cold.

Serves 6

> 1½ lb (700 g) lean minced beef
> 6 fl oz (175 ml) tomato juice
> 3–4 oz (75–100 g) porridge oats
> 1 egg, beaten
> 1 onion, chopped
> 1 tsp (5 ml) dried mixed herbs
> freshly ground pepper

Mix together all the ingredients, seasoning to taste with pepper. Line the base of a 2 lb (900 g) loaf tin with greaseproof paper. Put the meat mixture in the tin, level the top and bake in the oven at 190°C (375°F) mark 5 for about 1¼ hours. Turn out and cut into slices to serve.

Lamb Casserole

This warming casserole makes an ideal family supper for chilly days. Serve with warm crusty bread or jacket potatoes.

Serves 4–6

 1 lb (450 g) lean lamb, cubed
 1 oz (25 g) brown lentils or pot barley
 1 small onion, chopped
 ¾ pint (450 ml) tomato juice or stock
 8 oz (225 g) tomatoes, chopped
 8 oz (225 g) carrots, thinly sliced
 4 oz (100 g) fresh or frozen peas
 3 oz (75 g) mushrooms, sliced

Put the lamb in a saucepan and heat gently until browned on all sides, stirring occasionally. Add the lentils or barley, onion and tomato juice or stock, bring to the boil, then transfer to an ovenproof casserole. Cover and cook in the oven at 180°C (350°F) mark 4 for 1 hour. Add the tomatoes, carrots, peas and mushrooms and cook for a further 40 minutes or until all the vegetables and the meat are tender.

Lamb Meatballs

Serve these meatballs with Tomato Sauce (page 90) or in pitta bread pockets with shredded lettuce and sliced tomato or cucumber.

Makes 10–12

 2 oz (50 g) wholemeal breadcrumbs
 1 tbsp (15 ml) tomato purée
 12 oz (350 g) lean lamb, minced
 1 tbsp (15 ml) chopped fresh parsley
 1 small onion, chopped
 1 egg, beaten
 2 oz (50 g) plain wholemeal flour
 polyunsaturated oil, for frying

Mix together the breadcrumbs, tomato purée, lamb, parsley and onion with 1 tbsp (15 ml) water. Add enough egg to bind the ingredients together. Using floured hands, shape the mixture into small balls and coat in the flour. Heat a little oil in a non-stick frying pan and fry the meatballs for 10–12 minutes or until thoroughly cooked and golden brown. Drain on absorbent kitchen paper before serving.

Sunshine Liver

This unusual combination of liver and orange will tempt even unwilling liver-eaters! Serve with brown rice, or mashed or jacket potatoes.

Serves 4

> *12 oz (350 g) lamb's liver, thinly sliced*
> *3 tbsp (45 ml) plain wholemeal flour*
> *4 tbsp (60 ml) polyunsaturated oil*
> *1 medium onion, chopped*
> *½ pint (300 ml) Vegetable Stock (page 64)*
> *grated rind and juice of 1 orange*
> *½ tsp (2.5 ml) dried mixed herbs*

Toss the liver in the flour. Heat the oil in a saucepan and fry the liver gently for 5–7 minutes or until cooked through. Remove from the pan. Add the onion to the pan and cook for about 5 minutes or until soft, then stir in the stock, orange rind and juice and herbs. Bring to the boil, add the liver and simmer gently for 1 minute.

Liver Burgers

These burgers are an ideal way of getting children to eat liver. The mixture can also be shaped into croquettes. Serve them with jacket potatoes, vegetables or baked beans for a really nourishing meal.

Serves 6

8 oz (225 g) lamb's liver, roughly chopped
4 lean back bacon rashers, rinded and chopped
1 small onion, chopped
4 oz (100 g) wholemeal breadcrumbs
½ tsp (2.5 ml) dried mixed herbs (optional)
1 egg, beaten
polyunsaturated oil, for frying

Mix the liver, bacon and onion together and mince or chop finely in a blender or food processor. Transfer to a bowl and stir in half the breadcrumbs and the herbs, if using. Using floured hands, divide the mixture into six equal portions and shape into burgers or croquettes on a floured board. Chill in the refrigerator for about 1 hour or until firm.

Dip each burger or croquette in beaten egg and then coat with the remaining breadcrumbs. Heat a little oil in a non-stick frying pan and fry the burgers gently for 10–12 minutes or until cooked and golden. Drain on absorbent kitchen paper.

Ham and Tomato Quiche

Serves 6–8

8 oz (225 g) Wholemeal Shortcrust Pastry (page 149)
1 tbsp (15 ml) polyunsaturated oil
1 small onion, chopped
6 oz (175 g) lean ham, chopped
3 eggs
8 fl oz (225 ml) milk (whole, semi-skimmed or skimmed)
2 medium tomatoes, sliced
chopped fresh parsley, to garnish (optional)

Roll out the pastry on a lightly floured surface and use to line a 9 inch (23 cm) flan dish. Heat the oil in a frying pan and fry the onion gently for about 5 minutes or until soft. Combine the onion with the ham and place in the base of the pastry case.

Beat together the eggs and milk and pour into the flan case. Arrange slices of tomato on top. Bake in the oven at 200°C (400°F) mark 6 for 40–45 minutes or until the pastry is browned and the filling just set. Serve warm or cold.

Sausage and Bean Pie

Serves 3–4

8 oz (225 g) Home-made Sausages (page 107), reduced-fat
*   sausages or vegetarian sausages*
7 oz (200 g) can chopped tomatoes, drained
2–3 oz (50–75 g) fresh or frozen peas, cooked
3–4 oz (75–100 g) cooked red kidney beans or baked beans
1 lb (450 g) potatoes, cooked and mashed with a little
*   polyunsaturated margarine and milk*
tomato slices, to garnish

Grill the sausages for about 10 minutes or until brown and cooked through. Cut into chunks and put in the base of an ovenproof dish. Add the chopped tomatoes, peas and beans. Cover with a layer of mashed potato and bake in the oven at 190°C (375°F) mark 5 for 30–35 minutes or until the potato is golden brown. Garnish with tomato slices.

Fun food

Use slices of raw carrot, tomato or other vegetables and a few cooked kidney beans to make a face or pattern on top of the cooked pie.

Tomato Sauce

A healthy alternative to 'ketchup'.

Makes about ½ pint (300 ml)

14 oz (400 g) can chopped tomatoes
1 tbsp (15 ml) polyunsaturated oil
1 small onion, chopped
1 tsp (5 ml) vinegar
1 tsp (5 ml) Worcestershire sauce (optional)

Pour the tomatoes into a sieve and drain, discarding the juice. Heat the oil in a saucepan and gently fry the onion for about 5 minutes or until soft. Add the tomatoes and other ingredients and cook for a further 5 minutes, stirring occasionally. Remove from the heat, cool and purée until smooth.

Healthy Packed Lunches

Most children are happy with simple foods, such as sandwiches, fruit and yogurt, but it is worth providing some variety over the week. Remember that it is pointless if the packed lunch ends up in the bin and your child ends up in the chip shop, so make life easy for her by packing mostly food that can be eaten with the fingers (but do remember to pack cutlery if necessary). Find out whether your child will be provided with a drink and, if not, include some diluted fruit juice or a drink of milk.

Choose a container and contents that will withstand rough handling – you can buy children's lunchboxes or bags that are ideal; otherwise use a rigid plastic box with a lid, such as an ice-cream carton. Wrap food like sandwiches, rolls and cake in cling film (the new safer 'plasticizer-free' variety, if possible) or polythene bags, and use small airtight containers for things like salads. Small unbreakable flasks are the best choice for drinks and soup. Individual packs of food (small cartons of juice, boxes of raisins, and so on) cost more but score high on convenience and add extra interest to a packed lunch. Many supermarkets also stock mini-sized rolls and pitta breads which make life easier. There's no need to ban foods like crisps, biscuits and cakes from your child's lunchbox altogether, but don't include them everyday and choose healthier alternatives such as low-fat crisps, wholemeal scones or slices of teabread.

Packed Lunch Ideas

✻ Scrambled egg with cucumber or cress in a roll (preferably wholemeal), carton of natural or fruit yogurt, apple, small tub filled with sugar-free popcorn

✻ Wholemeal peanut butter sandwiches, cucumber sticks and a tomato, banana, carton of apple juice

✻ Herby Cheese Scones (page 138) filled with tomato or salad, two tangerines, small pack of nuts and raisins

✻ Slice of Ham and Tomato Quiche (page 89), mixed salad or vegetable sticks, wholemeal roll, a few dried apricots

✻ Cooked chicken drumstick, Fruity Coleslaw Salad (page 75), pitta bread, tomato, slice of Fruit Loaf (page 140)

✳ Small tub of Hummus (page 67) Sardine Dip (page 68) or other dip, vegetable sticks, bread sticks (Grissini), wholemeal pitta bread or crispbread, Muesli Bar (page 145), apple or pear

✳ French Bread Pizza (page 101), mixed salad or vegetable sticks, pot of natural or fruit-flavoured fromage frais

✳ Vegetable Pasty (page 116), carton of apple juice, dried fruit (such as raisins, no-soak dried apricots or stoned dates)

✳ Small flask of Lentil Soup (page 67), wholemeal roll, tub of cottage cheese with pineapple, packet of low-fat crisps, apple

Super Sandwiches

With a bit of imagination, even the simplest sandwiches can be transformed into fun food. The choice of breads and rolls is enormous – don't just stick to the sliced variety but try something different like rye or pitta bread for a change. All bread is nutritious, containing protein, energy and a range of nutrients, but the high fibre content of wholemeal bread makes it the healthiest choice. (Children reluctant to eat wholemeal bread will often eat sandwiches made with a slice of wholemeal and a slice of white bread.)

Stick to tiny two-bite sandwiches or shapes, such as animals, cut out with biscuit cutters for younger children. Choose simple fillings as toddlers usually like to know exactly what they are eating. Cheese, egg, lean meat, canned fish and peanut butter are popular and you can add thin slices of tomato, cucumber, grated carrot or apple, chopped watercress or salad cress for extra flavour. Older children can invent their own fillings. For packed lunches, choose a filling that won't make the bread soggy and don't overfill sandwiches or they will be difficult to handle. Save time by making a batch of sandwiches in advance, wrapping them individually and freezing. (Avoid fillings like egg and salad that don't freeze well.) Thaw for several hours or overnight in the refrigerator and add other ingredients, like salad, once thawed.

Pinwheels Cut the crusts off thin slices of bread. Spread with polyunsaturated margarine and filling to the edges, then carefully roll up each slice like a Swiss roll. Wrap each roll in cling film and chill. Cut rolls into slices approximately ½ inch (1 cm) thick and arrange on a plate.

Double Deckers Cut the crusts off thin slices of bread and spread with polyunsaturated margarine on one side. Layer three slices of bread together with a filling between each slice (use the same filling or two different types). Cut into fingers, squares or triangles.

Pyramids Cut the crusts off four thin slices of bread and trim into different-sized squares or circles, each one slightly smaller than the last. Spread with polyunsaturated margarine and filling and stack one on top of the other to form a pyramid.

Chequerboard Sandwiches Cut an equal number of thin slices of white and wholemeal bread. Cut off the crusts and spread with polyunsaturated margarine. Make up into sandwiches with one or more fillings. Cut each sandwich into four squares and arrange brown and white squares on a flat board or plate to resemble a chequerboard. (Top with a few pinwheel sandwiches, as above, to resemble draught pieces, if liked.)

Sandwich Shapes These are popular with younger children. Make up rounds of sandwiches and use a sharp knife to cut into simple shapes, such as triangles or diamonds. Alternatively, stamp out shapes, such as animals or people, using novelty biscuit cutters.

Open Sandwiches

Cut slices of bread or toast into fingers, squares or triangles or stamp out shapes with a cutter. Spread with polyunsaturated margarine and top with any type of filling. Decorate open sandwiches with slices of cucumber, tomato or other garnishes. Alternatively, use petit four cutters to stamp out tiny shapes from slices of ham, cheese or carrot and place on top. (If you have tiny alphabet cutters you could even spell out a message or your child's name!)

Funny Faces Stamp out rounds and spread with a smooth filling, such as soft cheese or peanut butter. Use pieces of tomato, radish or carrot for noses, eyes and mouths, and grated carrot or cress for hair.

Flower Sandwiches Stamp out rounds of bread using a small pluted pastry cutter. Spread with curd cheese and decorate with tiny bits of fruit or raisins.

Sandwich Fillings

Choose your child's favourite ingredients or try some of the following combinations:

Savoury Fillings

Cottage cheese Buy ready-flavoured varieties or add a small quantity of grated carrot, Cheddar cheese, finely chopped vegetables or salad.

Curd cheese or other medium- or low-fat soft cheese Flavour with ingredients as for cottage cheese. Alternatively, make spreads by blending equal quantities of curd cheese and ingredients such as sardines, tuna, cooked minced chicken or peanut butter.

Grated cheese Use plain grated cheese or flavour with a little grated onion, carrot, apple or chutney.

Egg Mash or finely chop hard-boiled eggs and combine with a little mayonnaise. Flavour with a little salad cress, chopped tomato or cucumber.

Sweet Fillings

Sugar-free fruit spreads Home-made thick fruit purées would be an even better alternative.

Sliced banana Use on their own or add thinly sliced dried dates.

Curd cheese or other medium- or low-fat soft cheese Flavour with a little chopped fresh or dried fruit (such as bananas, apple or no-soak dried apricots).

PASTA AND PANCAKES

Most children love pasta in one form or another and it is quick to prepare as well as brimming with goodness. Low in fat, with no added sugar or salt, it fits in neatly with ideas about healthy eating and provides growing children with protein, energy, iron and B vitamins. Wholewheat pasta is the best choice because it is naturally high in fibre, but all types of pasta are good for you. Served with one of the sauces below, or made up into dishes like Vegetable Lasagne (page 118), pasta makes an inexpensive and nourishing meal for all the family.

The pasta sauces below can be used for topping cooked pasta or as a filling for larger pasta shapes, such as cannelloni.

Fresh Tomato Sauce

Serves 4

> 1 tbsp (15 ml) polyunsaturated oil
> 1 small onion, chopped
> 1 lb (450 g) tomatoes, skinned and chopped, or one 14 oz
>   (400 g) can chopped tomatoes, drained
> 2 tbsp (30 ml) tomato purée
> ½ tsp (2.5 ml) dried oregano or mixed herbs

Heat the oil in a saucepan and fry the onion for about 5 minutes or until soft. Add the remaining ingredients, cover and simmer for about 15 minutes, stirring occasionally.

Variations

Tomato and Mushroom Sauce Add 2 oz (50 g) sliced mushrooms to the sauce with the tomatoes.

Tomato and Cheese Sauce Stir in 2 oz (50 g) grated Cheddar or Parmesan cheese just before serving.

Bolognese Sauce

Serves 4

> 1 tbsp (15 ml) polyunsaturated oil
> 1 small onion, chopped
> 2 carrots, finely chopped
> 1 small green or red pepper, peeled, cored, seeded and
>   chopped (optional)
> 8 oz (225 g) lean minced beef
> 14 oz (400 g) can chopped tomatoes
> 2 tbsp (30 ml) tomato purée
> ½–1 tsp (2.5–5 ml) dried mixed herbs

Heat the oil in a saucepan and gently fry the onion, carrots and pepper for about 5 minutes or until soft. Add the beef and cook for a further 10 minutes, stirring occasionally. Add the tomatoes, tomato purée and herbs and simmer gently for about 25 minutes or until the sauce is thick.

Tuna and Mushroom Sauce

Serves 4

> 1 tbsp (15 ml) polyunsaturated oil
> 3 oz (75 g) mushrooms, sliced
> 12 oz (350 g) tomatoes, skinned and chopped, or one 14 oz
>   (400 g) can chopped tomatoes, drained
> 1 tbsp (15 ml) tomato purée
> 7 oz (200 g) can tuna in brine, drained
> 1 tsp (5 ml) chopped fresh or dried parsley (optional)

Heat the oil in a saucepan and gently fry the mushrooms for about 5 minutes or until tender. Add the tomatoes and tomato purée and simmer for about 10 minutes. Flake the tuna and add to the tomato mixture with the parsley, if using. Cook for a further minute until hot.

Macaroni with Tuna

Serves 2–3

   4 oz (100 g) wholewheat macaroni
   1 oz (25 g) polyunsaturated margarine
   3 oz (75 g) onion, chopped
   ½ oz (15 g) cornflour
   ½ pint (300 ml) milk (whole, semi-skimmed or skimmed)
   1–2 tbsp (15–30 ml) tomato purée or ketchup
   3½ oz (115 g) can tuna in brine, drained and flaked
   2 oz (50 g) fresh or frozen peas, cooked
   1 oz (25 g) Cheddar cheese, grated

Cook the macaroni in boiling water for about 12 minutes or according to the directions on the packet. Drain well. Melt the margarine in a small saucepan, add the onion and fry for about 5 minutes or until soft. Blend the cornflour with a little of the milk, then stir in the remaining milk and add to the onion in the pan. Bring to the boil, stirring continuously. Remove from the heat and stir in the tomato purée or ketchup, tuna, peas and macaroni. Place in a heatproof dish, sprinkle with the cheese and cook under a moderate grill until bubbling and golden brown.

Pasta with Cottage Cheese and Vegetables

Choose any type of fresh pasta for this simple dish. Stuffed pasta, such as tortellini, can also be used.

Serves 4–6

   8 oz (225 g) fresh wholewheat pasta, eg. tagliatelli
   1 tbsp (15 ml) polyunsaturated oil
   4 oz (100 g) cooked or canned red kidney beans, drained
   4 oz (100 g) fresh or frozen peas, cooked
   8 oz (225 g) tub cottage cheese (plain or with chives)
   freshly ground pepper
   chopped fresh parsley, to garnish (optional)

Cook the pasta in boiling water for about 3 minutes or according to the directions on the packet. Drain well, return to the pan, add the oil and toss together. Stir in the beans, peas and cottage cheese and reheat briefly. Season with pepper and scatter with parsley, if liked. Serve immediately.

Pancakes

Pancakes are quick and easy to make and can be filled with sweet or savoury fillings. Wholemeal pancakes have a slightly heavier texture, so make them as thin as possible.

Makes 8

> *4 oz (100 g) plain unbleached white or wholemeal flour*
> *pinch of salt*
> *1 egg, beaten*
> *½ pint (300 ml) milk (whole, semi-skimmed or skimmed)*
> *polyunsaturated oil, for frying*

Sift the flour and salt into a mixing bowl. (If using wholemeal flour, return any bran left in the sieve to the bowl.) Make a well in the centre, pour in the egg and half the milk and stir, gradually incorporating the flour. Gradually beat in the remaining milk to form a smooth batter.

Heat a little oil in a 7 inch (18 cm) frying pan, tilting the pan gently to coat the base and sides with oil. Pour off any excess oil, then pour in just enough batter to coat the base of the pan very thinly. Cook for 1–2 minutes or until the underside is golden brown, then turn or toss and cook the other side. Transfer the pancake to a warm plate. Repeat with more batter, stacking the cooked pancakes with greaseproof paper between each one and keeping them warm in the oven. Alternatively, allow the stacked pancakes to cool, cover with cling film and refrigerate for up to 2 days, or freeze in a rigid container for up to 6 months. (Thaw before using.)

Pancake Fillings

Place a little of the filling along the centre of each pancake and roll up. Alternatively, fold each pancake in half, then in half again and open out to form a pocket for the filling.

Savoury Fillings

The following make enough filling for about eight pancakes:

Tomato and Courgette Heat 2 tbsp (30 ml) polyunsaturated oil in a saucepan and fry 8 oz (225 g) chopped onions until soft. Add a chopped green or red pepper and 8 oz (225 g) sliced courgettes and fry for 5 minutes. Add 8 oz (225 g) chopped tomatoes, 2 tbsp (30 ml) tomato purée, ¼ tsp (1.25 ml) dried oregano and a little pepper to taste. Cook for about 15 minutes or until tender.

Chinese Chicken Heat 1 tbsp (15 ml) polyunsaturated oil in a saucepan and fry 1 small chopped onion until soft. Add 2 oz (50 g) bean sprouts and 1 oz (25 g) thinly sliced mushrooms and cook for 2–3 minutes. Add 5 oz (150 g) drained canned (or cooked frozen) sweetcorn and 8 oz (225 g) diced cooked chicken meat. Cook until thoroughly heated and stir in a little soy sauce to taste.

Sweet Fillings

The simplest way to serve pancakes sweet is with freshly squeezed lemon juice or a little pure fruit juice. Sweeten with just a little honey or sugar, if necessary. Pancakes are also delicious spread with fruit purées or sugar-free jam and rolled up. The following make enough filling for about eight pancakes:

Mixed Fruit Stew 1½ lb (700 g) prepared fruits (eg. peeled and cored apples or pears, rhubarb, plums, peaches or apricots, with a little water or fruit juice until soft. Sweeten to taste with a little sugar or honey, if necessary.

Apricot Soak 8 oz (225 g) dried apricots overnight in water or apple juice. Stew gently for about 10 minutes, then purée in a blender or food processor.

Dutch Apple Stew 1½ lb (700 g) peeled and cored cooking apples in a little water. Sweeten to taste with sugar or honey, if necessary. Stir in ½ tsp (2.5 ml) ground cinnamon and 2–3 oz (50–75 g) sultanas or raisins.

Fruit and Yogurt Mix 12 fl oz (350 ml) Greek-style natural yogurt with 12 oz (350 g) chopped or sliced fresh fruits (eg. strawberries, apples, bananas, grapes, oranges, pears or raspberries).

FAST FOODS

Convenience foods can be a Godsend for busy parents and provide a fast and easy way of feeding the family. The problem is that many convenience foods and take-aways are high in fat, salt and additives and low in fibre. The other problem is that there is seldom any way of knowing exactly what you are buying. How can you tell how much fish is in a fishcake or how much beef is in a beefburger? Even if a list of ingredients on the packet tells you, for example, how much beef is in a burger, it is misleading because what can legally be described as lean beef may actually consist partly of fat and gristle, or of meats other than beef.

It's not all doom and gloom, however. If you rely on convenience foods, there are plenty of reasonably healthy ones to choose from – pizza, jacket potatoes, sandwiches, fish fingers, frozen vegetables, canned or dried beans and fruit in fruit juice, for instance. Try to balance the amount of convenience foods you eat with plenty of fresh fruit, vegetables and whole grain cereals.

Food manufacturers are gradually responding to current ideas about healthy eating by producing at least some foods with less fat, sugar and salt and fewer additives, and many include helpful nutritional information on their labels, giving consumers a better idea of what they are eating.

The recipes in this section are healthy home-made versions of popular convenience foods – they may not taste exactly the same as shop-bought foods but they are much healthier and you will know exactly what they contain.

French Bread Pizzas

Quick and easy to make, these mini-pizzas are delicious hot or cold and ideal for picnics, parties and lunchboxes.

Makes 4

10 inch (25 cm) length of French bread stick, preferably
*   wholemeal*
1 tbsp (15 ml) vegetable oil
1 small onion, chopped
10 oz (275 g) canned chopped tomatoes, drained
2 tbsp (30 ml) tomato purée
1 tsp (5 ml) dried oregano or mixed herbs
4 oz (100 g) Cheddar cheese, grated
1 oz (25 g) mushrooms, thinly sliced
2 tomatoes, sliced

Cut the French stick in half lengthways, then cut each half across the middle. Place on a baking sheet. Heat the oil in a saucepan and fry the onion for about 5 minutes or until soft. Add the tomatoes, tomato purée and herbs. Cook for a further 5 minutes, stirring occasionally. Spoon some of the tomato mixture on to each piece of bread and spread to the edges. Top with grated cheese and arrange sliced mushrooms and tomatoes on top. Bake in the oven at 200°C (400°F) mark 6 for 15–20 minutes or until bubbling and golden brown.

Beefburgers (Quarter-pounders)

Serves 4

1 lb (450 g) lean minced beef
1 small onion, finely chopped
1 tsp (5 ml) dried mixed herbs
freshly ground pepper
a little polyunsaturated oil
4 wholemeal baps, halved horizontally
2 tomatoes, sliced
shredded lettuce

101

Mix together the beef, onion and herbs and season to taste with pepper. Using floured hands, shape the mixture into four balls and flatten into burger shapes. Chill until required.

Brush the burgers with oil and cook under a moderate grill for 10–12 minutes, turning once. Place a burger in each bap, add some tomato slices and shredded lettuce, and serve at once.

Note

To serve six, use the same mixture to make smaller burgers, but remember to reduce the cooking time.

Fish Fingers

Shop-bought fish fingers can consist of as little as one-third fish, and may contain additives such as colourings and poly-phosphates along with added water. These home-made fish fingers are just as good to eat, better value for money and better for your children.

Makes 6–8

> *8 oz (225 g) white fish fillets, skinned*
> *2 oz (50 g) wholemeal breadcrumbs*
> *½ oz (15 g) sesame seeds*
> *1 egg, beaten*
> *2 tsp (10 ml) polyunsaturated oil*

Cut the fish into fingers about 1 × 4 inches (2.5 × 10 cm). Mix together the breadcrumbs and sesame seeds. Beat together the egg and oil and pour into a shallow dish. Dip each fish finger first into the breadcrumb mixture, then into the egg, then once again into the breadcrumbs until evenly coated. Place on a lightly oiled baking sheet and bake in the oven at 180°C (350°F) mark 4 for 15–20 minutes or until cooked through and golden brown, turning once.

Quick Pizza

This pizza is quick and easy to prepare and is delicious hot or cold.

Serves 4–6

FOR THE BASE
8 oz (225 g) self-raising wholemeal flour
½ tsp (2.5 ml) salt
2 oz (50 g) polyunsaturated margarine
¼ pint (150 ml) milk

FOR THE TOPPING
2 tbsp (30 ml) polyunsaturated oil
1 small onion, chopped
4 tbsp (60 ml) tomato purée
2 tomatoes, chopped
½ tsp (2.5 ml) dried mixed herbs
freshly ground pepper
4 oz (100 g) Cheddar or medium-fat Mozzarella cheese, thinly sliced
2 oz (50 g) mushrooms, thinly sliced
2 tomatoes, sliced

Sift the flour and salt into a bowl and add any bran left in the sieve. Rub in the margarine until the mixture resembles breadcrumbs. Add the milk and mix to form a soft dough. Knead lightly on a floured surface, then roll out to a round approximately 9 inches (23 cm) in diameter. Place on a lightly oiled baking sheet.

Heat the oil in a saucepan and fry the onion for about 5 minutes or until soft. Stir in the tomato purée, chopped tomatoes, herbs and pepper to taste. Cook for about 5 minutes or until thickened. Spread the tomato mixture on top of the pizza base. Top with the cheese slices and mushrooms and finish with tomato slices. Bake in the oven at 220°C (425°F) mark 7 for about 25 minutes or until well risen and golden. Cut into wedges to serve.

Oven Chips

These chunky chips are lower in fat than ordinary chips. Cut into different shapes with a sharp knife or stamp out shapes with small biscuit cutters.

Serves 3–4

> *1 lb (450 g) potatoes, thickly sliced*
> *2 tbsp (30 ml) polyunsaturated oil*

Cut the potato slices into chunky chip shapes, or into other shapes with biscuit cutters. Heat the oil in a large roasting tin and add the potato shapes. Turn to coat evenly with oil, then bake in the oven at 200°C (400°F) mark 6 for about 30 minutes or until crisp and golden on the outside and soft inside, turning once. Drain on absorbent kitchen paper and serve immediately.

Bean Feasts

Canned baked beans are popular with children and their low-fat, high-fibre content makes them a good choice. Look for those with lower levels of sugar and salt.

Serves 2–3

> *14 oz (400 g) can baked beans*
> *wholemeal bread or toast, to serve*

Heat the beans in a saucepan. Add one of the following flavourings and heat thoroughly. Serve on wholemeal toast.

Flavourings

Curry Stir in ½–1 tsp (2.5–5 ml) mild curry powder and 1 oz (25 g) sultanas.

Cheese and Onion Skin and chop a small onion and fry gently in 1 tsp (5 ml) polyunsaturated oil for about 5 minutes or until soft. Stir into the hot beans with 2 oz (50 g) grated Cheddar cheese.

Sausage Add two thickly sliced cooked low-fat chipolata sausages, Home-made Sausages (page 107) or Vegebangers.

Ham and Herb Add 2 oz (50 g) cooked lean ham and ½ tsp (2.5 ml) dried mixed herbs.

Jacket Potatoes

Choose fairly large even-shaped potatoes. Cook the potatoes in a conventional oven or microwave cooker if you have one. (Follow the microwave cooker manufacturer's recommended cooking and standing times.)

Serves 4

4 baking potatoes, each weighing 7–8 oz (200–225 g)
a little polyunsaturated margarine
a little milk

Scrub the potatoes and prick all over with a fork. Bake the potatoes in the oven at 200°C (400°F) mark 6 for about 1½ hours or until the centres are cooked and the potatoes feel soft when squeezed. Cut each potato in half and carefully scoop out the flesh into a large bowl, leaving the skins intact. Mash the potato with enough margarine and milk to give a smooth consistency. Leave the potato plain or combine with one of the following fillings. Pile the potato back into the reserved skins, place on a baking sheet and cook for a further 20 minutes or until piping hot and golden brown.

Fillings

Plain Add a little salt and pepper to taste. Sprinkle with chopped fresh chives or parsley just before serving.

Cheese and Chutney Add 4 oz (100 g) grated Cheddar cheese and 3 tbsp (45 ml) chutney to the mashed potato.

Bacon, Mushroom and Onion Heat 1 tsp (5 ml) polyunsaturated oil in a frying pan and gently fry 3 oz (75 g) chopped lean bacon, 1 small chopped onion and 4 oz (100 g) chopped mushrooms for about 5 minutes or until soft. Stir into the mashed potato.

Mixed Vegetable Stir in 5 oz (125 g) cooked or drained canned sweetcorn, 4 oz (100 g) cooked red kidney beans, 2–3 tbsp (30–45 ml) Greek-style natural yogurt, 2 tsp (10 ml) chopped fresh parsley.

Quick Chilli Con Carne
Serves 3–4

> 1 tbsp (15 ml) polyunsaturated oil
> 1 medium onion, chopped
> 1 medium green pepper, cored, seeded and chopped
> 7 oz (200 g) lean minced beef
> 2–3 fl oz (50–75 ml) stock or water
> 14 oz (400 g) can baked beans (preferably the reduced-sugar variety)
> ½–1 tsp (2.5–5 ml) chilli powder
> cooked brown rice, to serve

Heat the oil in a saucepan. Add the onion, pepper and mince and fry gently for about 5 minutes, stirring occasionally. Pour in the stock or water and simmer for 10 minutes. Add the baked beans and chilli powder, stir well and cook for a further 10 minutes. Serve with brown rice.

Vegeburgers
Makes 6

> polyunsaturated oil, for frying
> 1 onion, chopped
> 6 oz (175 g) Cheddar or Edam cheese, finely chopped
> 5 oz (150 g) mixed nuts, chopped (eg. walnuts, hazelnuts, almonds, brazils)
> 7 oz (200 g) wholemeal breadcrumbs
> 2 small carrots, grated
> ½ tsp (2.5 ml) dried mixed herbs (optional)
> 2 eggs, beaten
> 1 oz (25 g) plain wholemeal flour

Heat 1 tbsp (15 ml) oil in a frying pan, add the onion and fry gently for about 5 minutes or until soft. Place the onion, cheese, nuts, 6 oz (175 g) breadcrumbs, the carrots and herbs in a bowl and mix well. Bind the mixture with about half the beaten egg. Divide the mixture into six and, using floured hands, form into burger shapes. Mix the flour with the remaining breadcrumbs and spread on a large plate.

Dip each burger, first into the remaining egg, then into the flour and breadcrumb mixture to coat. Heat a little oil in a large frying pan, add the burgers and fry over a moderate heat for about 15 minutes or until cooked through and golden brown, turning once. Drain on absorbent kitchen paper before serving.

Fun food

Serve the burgers in wholemeal rolls with some shredded salad or Fruity Coleslaw Salad (page 75).

Home-made Sausages

These sausages are simple to make and are ideal cold for picnics and lunchboxes.

Makes 16

> 1 lb (450 g) lean pork, turkey or chicken, minced
> 6 oz (175 g) wholemeal breadcrumbs
> ½ tsp (2.5 ml) dried mixed herbs
> 2 tsp (10 ml) tomato purée (optional)
> 1 small onion, very finely chopped
> 1 egg, beaten
> polyunsaturated oil, for grilling

Mix together the minced meat, breadcrumbs, herbs, tomato purée and chopped onion. Add enough of the egg to bind the ingredients together, adding a little flour to the mixture if it becomes too sticky. Form into a ball and turn on to a well floured board. Divide the mixture into 16 equal portions and shape each one into a sausage shape. Brush with a little oil and cook under a moderate grill for 10–15 minutes or until cooked through and golden brown. Serve hot or cold.

Fun food

To make home-made hot dogs, split open small wholemeal rolls, add some salad or shredded vegetables and pop in a cooked sausage. Serve in a paper napkin instead of on a plate.

Chinese Chicken

Serves 4

> *3 tbsp (45 ml) polyunsaturated oil*
> *2 small onions, chopped*
> *3 oz (75 g) mushrooms, sliced*
> *1 small green pepper, cored, seeded and chopped*
> *1 lb (450 g) chicken breast meat, skinned and cut into small*
>   *strips or cubes*
> *1 tbsp (15 ml) cornflour*
> *1 tbsp (15 ml) soy sauce*
> *1 tbsp (15 ml) crunchy peanut butter*
> *½ pint (300 ml) Vegetable Stock (page 64)*
> *3 oz (75 g) bean sprouts*
> *boiled brown rice or noodles, to serve*

Heat the oil in a saucepan and fry the onions, mushrooms and pepper for about 5 minutes or until soft. Remove from the pan with a slotted spoon and reserve. Toss the chicken in the cornflour and fry in the oil remaining in the pan for 5 minutes or until browned. Mix together the soy sauce, peanut butter and stock. Return the vegetables to the pan with the stock mixture and bean sprouts and simmer for about 15 minutes. Serve with rice or noodles.

Pitta Pockets

Makes 8 pockets

> *4 wholemeal pitta breads*
> *4 oz (100 g) frozen sweetcorn, cooked*
> *3½ oz (90 g) can tuna in brine, drained and flaked*
> *1 oz (25 g) Cheddar cheese, cubed*
> *2 inch (5 cm) piece of cucumber, peeled and chopped*
> *shredded lettuce*

Cut each pitta bread in half crossways and open out to form pockets. Mix together the sweetcorn, tuna, cheese and cucumber. Put a little shredded lettuce into each pocket and top with some of the sweetcorn mixture.

MEATLESS MEALS

A vegetarian diet can be perfectly healthy for children of all ages. If anything, vegetarians tend to be healthier than those who eat meat. Meat is not essential – meals based on vegetables, fruits, cereals, pulses and nuts can provide children with all the protein and other nutrients they need – and they are usually cheaper too.

The following recipes include some vegetable accompaniments, as well as vegetarian main dishes to serve for lunch or supper.

Macaroni Cheese

Any type of small pasta shapes (such as twists or rings) can be used in place of the macaroni.

Serves 4–6

6 oz (175 g) wholewheat short-cut macaroni
1½ oz (40 g) polyunsaturated margarine
4 tbsp (60 ml) plain wholemeal flour
1 pint (568 ml) milk (whole, semi-skimmed or skimmed)
5 oz (150 g) Cheddar cheese, grated
tomato slices, to garnish

Cook the macaroni in boiling water for about 12 minutes, or according to the instructions on the packet. Drain well.

Melt the margarine in a saucepan and stir in the flour. Cook for 2 minutes, stirring to prevent sticking. Remove the pan from the heat and gradually stir in the milk. Bring to the boil and cook for 2 minutes, stirring all the time, until the sauce is thick and smooth. Add 4 oz (100 g) of the cheese and stir until melted, then add the macaroni. Pour into an ovenproof dish and sprinkle over the remaining cheese. Bake in the oven at 200°C (400°F) mark 6 for about 20 minutes or until bubbling and golden. Garnish with tomato slices before serving.

109

Cheesy Bean Pie

Serves 4

good pinch of dried mixed herbs (optional)
2–3 oz (50–75 g) Cheddar cheese, grated
1½ lb (700 g) potatoes, boiled and mashed with a little
 polyunsaturated margarine and milk
1 tsp (5 ml) polyunsaturated oil
1 small onion, chopped
4 oz (100 g) frozen peas or mixed vegetables
6 oz (175 g) cooked beans (eg. red kidney or butter beans)
14 oz (400 g) can chopped tomatoes, drained

Beat the herbs and cheese into the mashed potato. Heat the oil
in a small frying pan and fry the onion for about 5 minutes or
until soft. Mix together the onion, peas, beans and tomatoes and
spoon into an ovenproof dish. Top with a layer of mashed potato
and bake in the oven at 190°C (375°F) mark 5 for about 35
minutes or until golden brown.

Cheese Sauce

Makes about ½ pint (300 ml)

½ oz (15 g) polyunsaturated margarine
½ oz (15 g) plain flour
½ pint (300 ml) milk (whole, semi-skimmed or skimmed)
2 oz (50 g) Cheddar cheese, grated
freshly ground pepper

Melt the margarine in a saucepan, stir in the flour and cook for
1 minute, stirring. Remove from the heat and gradually stir in
the milk. Bring to the boil, stirring continuously, and cook for a
further 2 minutes or until the sauce is thick and smooth. Remove
from the heat and add cheese, stirring until melted. Season to
taste with pepper.

Variation

Cheese and Herb Sauce Add ½ tsp (2.5 ml) dried mixed herbs
or 1 tsp (5 ml) chopped fresh mixed herbs with the cheese.

Cheese and Vegetable Layer

Serves 4

    8 oz (225 g) potatoes, boiled
    4–6 oz (100–175 g) frozen mixed vegetables, cooked
    ½ pint (300 ml) Cheese Sauce (page 110)
    2 oz (50 g) wholemeal breadcrumbs
    1 oz (25 g) Cheddar cheese, grated

Cut the cooked potatoes into bite-sized cubes and combine with the mixed vegetables. Place in a 1 pint (600 ml) ovenproof dish and pour over the cheese sauce. Mix together the breadcrumbs and cheese and sprinkle over the top. Bake in the oven at 190°C (375°F) mark 5 for 35–40 minutes.

Cheesy Bread and Butter Pudding

Serves 2–3

    3 thick slices of bread, preferably wholemeal
    polyunsaturated margarine, for spreading
    2 oz (50 g) Cheddar or Edam cheese, grated
    ½ pint (300 ml) milk (whole, semi-skimmed or skimmed)
    2 eggs, beaten

Remove the crusts from the bread, spread thinly with margarine and cut each slice into quarters. Lightly grease a 1 pint (600 ml) ovenproof dish and arrange the bread and grated cheese in layers, reserving a little of the cheese.

Heat the milk until hot but not boiling. Pour on to the beaten eggs, stirring all the time. Pour the egg mixture over the bread and sprinkle with the remaining cheese. Bake in the oven at 190°C (375°F) mark 5 for about 35 minutes or until set and golden brown.

Simple Soufflé

Served with a salad and some wholemeal bread, this quick and easy soufflé makes a nourishing family supper.

1 oz (25 g) polyunsaturated margarine
2 tbsp (30 ml) plain flour
8 fl oz (225 ml) milk (whole, semi-skimmed or skimmed)
4 eggs, separated
3 oz (75 g) Cheddar cheese, grated
freshly ground pepper

Melt the margarine in a saucepan, add the flour and cook gently for 1 minute, stirring. Remove from the heat and gradually stir in the milk. Bring to the boil, stirring continuously, and cook for a further 2 minutes or until the sauce is smooth and thick. Remove from the heat, cool slightly, then beat in the egg yolks. Stir in the cheese and season to taste with pepper.

Whisk the egg whites until stiff and fold gently into the sauce until just evenly mixed. Pour into a greased 2½ pint (1.4 litre) soufflé dish and bake in the oven at 180°C (350°F) mark 4 for about 30 minutes or until well risen and golden brown.

Oaty Sweetcorn Quiche

Serves 6

4 oz (100 g) plain wholemeal flour
4 oz (100 g) oatmeal
4 oz (100 g) polyunsaturated margarine
1 tbsp (15 ml) polyunsaturated oil
1 small onion, chopped
12 oz (350 g) can sweetcorn, drained
4 oz (100 g) Cheddar cheese, grated
3 eggs, beaten
½ pint (300 ml) milk (whole, semi-skimmed or skimmed)

Mix together the flour and oatmeal in a bowl. Rub in the margarine until the mixture resembles fine breadcrumbs. Add 2–3 tbsp (30–45 ml) water and mix to a firm dough. Knead lightly on a floured surface, then roll out and use to line an 8 inch (20.5 cm) flan dish.

Heat the oil in a small saucepan and fry the onion for 5 minutes or until soft. Place the onion and sweetcorn in the base of the flan and sprinkle over the grated cheese. Beat together the eggs and milk and pour into the flan. Bake at 190°C (375°F) mark 5 for 40–45 minutes or until set and golden brown.

Pea and Leek Quiche

Serves 6–8

> *1 lb (450 g) leeks, thinly sliced*
> *8 oz (225 g) Wholemeal Shortcrust Pastry (page 149)*
> *4 oz (100 g) fresh or frozen peas, cooked*
> *½ pint (300 ml) milk (whole, semi-skimmed or skimmed)*
> *2 large eggs, beaten*
> *freshly ground pepper*
> *2–3 oz (50–75 g) Cheddar cheese, grated (optional)*

Cook the leeks in a little boiling water for about 10 minutes or until just tender. Drain well. Roll out the pastry on a lightly floured surface and use to line an 8 inch (20.5 cm) flan dish. Put the leeks and peas in the base of the pastry case.

Beat together the milk and eggs and season to taste with pepper. Pour over the vegetables. Sprinkle the grated cheese on top, if using, and bake in the oven at 190°C (375°F) mark 5 for 40–45 minutes or until golden brown and set. Serve hot or cold.

Potato Nests

Serves 4

> *1 lb (450 g) potatoes, boiled and mashed with a little*
> *polyunsaturated margarine and milk*
> *4 tbsp (60 ml) cooked beans (eg. kidney, flageolet or butter*
> *beans) or baked beans*
> *2 oz (50 g) Cheddar cheese, grated*
> *tomato slices and salad cress, to garnish*

Divide the mashed potato in four and place in mounds on a large ovenproof plate. Form into rounds, flatten slightly and make a small well in the centre of each. Mark with a fork to resemble a nest. Place some of the cooked beans in the centre of each nest, top with a little cheese and cook under a moderate grill until the cheese is bubbling and beginning to brown. Garnish with tomato slices and cress before serving.

Fun food

Instead of garnishing with tomato slices, place two or three tiny cherry tomatoes on top of each nest to resemble eggs.

Lentil Dal

Serves 4–6

> *2 tbsp (30 ml) polyunsaturated oil*
> *1 onion, chopped*
> *8 oz (225 g) split red lentils*
> *¾ pint (450 ml) Vegetable Stock (page 64) or water*
> *1–2 tsp (5–10 ml) mild curry paste (optional)*
> *wholemeal pitta bread, to serve*

Heat the oil in a saucepan and gently fry the onion for about 5 minutes or until soft. Add the remaining ingredients, bring to the boil, cover and simmer gently for about 20 minutes or until the lentils are tender. Remove from the heat and beat with a wooden spoon until smooth. Serve with warm wholemeal pitta bread.

Potato Layer

Serves 4–6

> *1¼ lb (550 g) potatoes, thinly sliced*
> *¼ pint (150 ml) hot Vegetable Stock (page 64) or milk*
> *½ oz (15 g) polyunsaturated margarine*

Layer the potatoes in a shallow ovenproof dish. Pour over the hot stock or milk and dot with margarine. Cover and bake in the oven at 190°C (375°F) mark 5 for about 30 minutes. Uncover and cook for a further 45 minutes or until the potatoes are tender and golden brown on top.

Roast Jacket Potatoes

Serves 6

> 1–1½ lb (450–700 g) medium potatoes
> 1–2 tbsp (15–30 ml) polyunsaturated oil

Scrub the potatoes and cut into chunks about 1 inch (2.5 cm) square. Put the oil in a roasting tin and heat in the oven at 220°C (425°F) mark 7. Add the potatoes and turn so they are completely coated with oil. Bake for about 1 hour, turning occasionally, until soft in the centre and crisp and golden on the outside.

Vegetable Bake

A good way to get children to eat vegetables is to serve them in disguise. This savoury bake is often popular with children who usually refuse to eat vegetables.

Serves 4

> 2 tsp (10 ml) vegetable oil
> 1 medium onion, finely chopped
> 1½ lb (700 g) carrots, sliced
> 4 fl oz (100 ml) Vegetable Stock (page 64)
> 4 oz (100 g) fresh or frozen peas
> 2 eggs
> 2 oz (50 g) curd cheese
> ½ tsp (2.5 ml) dried mixed herbs (optional)

Heat the oil in a saucepan over a low heat, add the onion and cook for about 5 minutes or until soft. Add the carrots and cook for a further 2–3 minutes to seal in the flavour. Add the stock, cover the pan tightly and cook over a low heat for about 20 minutes or until tender. Add the peas and cook for a further 5 minutes. Strain the vegetables, then mince or coarsely chop in a food processor.

Beat the eggs and stir into the curd cheese with the herbs, if using. Stir into the vegetable mixture. Lightly oil a 1½ pint (900 ml) ovenproof dish and spoon in the mixture. Level the surface, then bake in the oven at 190°C (375°F) mark 5 for 40–45 minutes or until firm. Serve hot or cold.

Vegetable Pasties

These substantial pasties are ideal for packed lunches and picnics.

Makes 4 large pasties

> *8 oz (225 g) mixed root vegetables (eg. potatoes, carrots and swede)*
> *2 oz (50 g) cooked peas or beans (eg. red kidney or butter beans)*
> *4 oz (100 g) Cheddar cheese, grated*
> *½ tsp (2.5 ml) dried oregano or mixed herbs*
> *1 lb (450 g) Wholemeal Shortcrust Pastry (page 149)*
> *a little milk, to glaze*

Mix together the vegetables, cheese and herbs. Roll out the pastry on a lightly floured surface and cut out four 7 inch (18 cm) rounds. Spoon some of the filling into the centre of each round. Brush the edges of the pastry with milk and bring together over the filling to form pasties. Pinch or crimp the edges to seal.

Place the pasties on a baking sheet, brush with milk and bake in the oven at 200°C (400°F) mark 6 for 15 minutes, then reduce the heat to 180°C (350°F) mark 4 and cook for a further 20–25 minutes or until the vegetables are tender when a sharp knife is inserted. Serve hot or cold.

Vegetable Curry

Children with more adventurous tastes often enjoy mildly spiced food like this curry. Serve with boiled brown rice and other accompaniments such as Yogurt and Cucumber Salad (page 76), chopped apple or banana slices (dip in lemon juice to prevent browning) or wholemeal chappatis.

Serves 4–6

> *1 tbsp (15 ml) polyunsaturated oil*
> *1 large onion, chopped*
> *4 tsp (20 ml) plain wholemeal flour*
> *½ pint (300 ml) Vegetable Stock (page 64)*
> *3 medium potatoes, diced*

116

1 large carrot, thickly sliced
½ cauliflower, broken into florets
4 tomatoes, skinned and chopped
8 oz (225 g) cooked red kidney beans
4 oz (100 g) frozen peas
1–2 tbsp (15–30 ml) mild curry paste
¼ pint (150 ml) Greek-style natural yogurt
1 tbsp (15 ml) tomato purée
boiled brown rice, to serve

Heat the oil in a saucepan and fry the onion for about 5 minutes or until soft. Add the flour and cook for a further 2 minutes, stirring occasionally. Remove from the heat and gradually stir in the stock. Add the potatoes, carrot, cauliflower and tomatoes, cover and simmer for about 20 minutes or until the vegetables are tender. Add the kidney beans and peas and cook for a further 5 minutes, adding a little extra water if the mixture becomes too dry.

Mix together the curry paste, yogurt and tomato purée, then add to the vegetable mixture and cook for 2 minutes, stirring to prevent sticking. Serve with rice and other accompaniments.

Winter Vegetable Hotpot

Serves 3–4

1 small onion, chopped
12 oz (350 g) potatoes, cubed
8 oz (225 g) swede, diced
2 oz (50 g) frozen peas
3 carrots, thinly sliced
2 small leeks, sliced
2 tsp (10 ml) yeast extract
½ pint (300 ml) hot Vegetable Stock (page 64) or water
4 oz (100 g) Cheddar cheese, grated

Put the vegetables, yeast extract and stock into a saucepan, bring to the boil and simmer for about 30 minutes or until the vegetables are tender. Transfer to a heatproof dish, top with the grated cheese and put under a moderate grill for about 5 minutes or until bubbling and just beginning to brown.

Vegetable Lasagne
Serves 6–8

> 10 sheets dried lasagne (wholewheat, egg or spinach)
> 3 tbsp (45 ml) polyunsaturated oil
> 2 medium onions, chopped
> 8 oz (225 g) mushrooms, sliced
> 12 oz (350 g) courgettes, sliced
> 2 tsp (10 ml) dried oregano
> 1 lb (450 g) tomatoes, chopped
> 3 tbsp (45 ml) tomato purée
> fresh parsley sprigs and tomato slices, to garnish

> FOR THE CHEESE SAUCE
> 1 oz (25 g) polyunsaturated margarine
> 1 oz (25 g) plain flour
> 1 pint (568 ml) milk (whole, semi-skimmed or skimmed)
> 4 oz (100 g) Cheddar cheese, grated

Cook the lasagne in boiling water for 10–15 minutes or according to the directions on the packet. Drain well. Heat the oil in a saucepan and gently fry the onions for about 5 minutes or until soft. Add the mushrooms and courgettes and cook for a further 5 minutes. Add the oregano, tomatoes and tomato purée, cover and cook for a further 15 minutes, stirring occasionally.

For the cheese sauce, melt the margarine in a saucepan, stir in the flour and cook for 1 minute, stirring. Remove from the heat and gradually stir in the milk. Return to the heat, stirring all the time until the sauce comes to the boil and thickens. Remove from the heat and stir in 3 oz (75 g) of the cheese.

Lightly oil a 4 pint (2.3 litre) ovenproof dish. Spoon in some of the vegetable mixture, cover with a layer of lasagne and spread over a layer of cheese sauce. Repeat these layers, ending with a layer of cheese sauce. Sprinkle the remaining cheese on top and bake in the oven at 180°C (350°F) mark 4 for about 45 minutes or until bubbling and golden. Garnish with parsley sprigs and tomato slices.

Nut Roast

Serves 4–6

6 oz (175 g) mixed nuts (eg. walnuts, peanuts, brazils,
   cashews or almonds), chopped
3 oz (75 g) wholemeal breadcrumbs
1 tsp (5 ml) dried oregano
1 tbsp (15 ml) polyunsaturated oil
1 large onion, chopped
1 tsp (5 ml) yeast extract
6 fl oz (175 ml) hot water
2 large tomatoes
3 oz (75 g) Cheddar cheese, grated

Mix together the nuts, breadcrumbs and oregano. Heat the oil
in a small frying pan and fry the onion for about 5 minutes or
until soft. Dissolve the yeast extract in the water and add to the
nut mixture with the onion.

Grease a 1 lb (450 g) loaf tin and line the base with greaseproof paper. Place half the mixture in the tin and layer the
tomatoes and cheese on top. Place the rest of the nut mixture
on top, pressing down well. Bake in the oven at 190°C (375°F)
mark 5 for about 50 minutes. Leave in the tin for a few minutes
before turning out.

Vegetable Risotto

Serves 4

8 oz (225 g) easy-cook long grain brown rice
1 small onion, chopped
14 oz (400 g) can chopped tomatoes
1 tbsp (15 ml) tomato purée
1 tsp (5 ml) dried oregano
1 pint (600 ml) Vegetable Stock (page 64) or tomato juice
2 oz (50 g) mushrooms, chopped
2 oz (50 g) fresh or frozen peas, cooked
2 oz (50 g) cooked frozen or canned sweetcorn, drained

119

Put the rice, onion, tomatoes, tomato purée, oregano and stock in a saucepan. Bring to the boil, then simmer gently for 25–30 minutes or until the rice is tender, adding a little extra stock or water if necessary. Add the mushrooms, peas and sweetcorn a few minutes before the end of cooking.

Variation

Cheese and Vegetable Risotto Sprinkle 2–3 oz (50–75 g) grated Cheddar cheese over the risotto just before serving. Garnish with sliced tomatoes.

Egg, Potato and Tomato Bake

Serves 4–6

> *4 eggs*
> *1 pint (568 ml) milk (whole, semi-skimmed or skimmed)*
> *1 lb (450 g) cooked potatoes, sliced*
> *8 oz (225 g) tomatoes, sliced*
> *6 oz (175 g) Cheddar cheese, grated*
> *tomato slices, to garnish*

Beat together the eggs and milk. Layer the potatoes, tomatoes and cheese in an ovenproof casserole, reserving a little cheese. Pour over the egg mixture and sprinkle the reserved cheese on top. Bake in the oven at 180°C (350°F) mark 4 for about 40 minutes or until the mixture has set and the top is brown. Garnish with tomato slices just before serving.

PERFECT PUDDINGS

Puddings are not essential but most children enjoy something sweet to end a meal. Fresh fruit or yogurt (choose sugar-free varieties with no additives) are simple and healthy choices for a dessert, and popular with children of all ages. Manufactured desserts tend to be high in fat and sugar. There is no need to ban sugary foods altogether, but keep them to a minimum and serve them at mealtimes so they are less likely to damage teeth. Make your own puddings whenever you can, using healthy ingredients like wholemeal flour and polyunsaturated fat, and use as little sugar as possible.

Fruity Kebabs

Make these little kebabs with bite-sized pieces of your child's favourite fruits. Use fresh fruit or canned fruits in fruit juice (or a mixture of both). Toss bananas and apples in lemon juice to prevent browning.

Makes 4

> 1 small banana
> 1 tbsp (15 ml) lemon juice
> 1 small eating apple, peeled and cored
> 8 seedless grapes
> 8 strawberries, hulled
> 2 oz (50 g) peach slices in natural juice, drained

Peel and thickly slice the banana and toss in lemon juice. Cut the apples into bite-sized cubes and toss in lemon juice. Wash and pat dry the grapes and strawberries. Cut each peach slice in half across the middle. Thread the fruits on to four plastic drinking straws, piercing a hole with a skewer first if necessary. Serve immediately.

Variation

Dried Fruit Kebabs Use a mixture of dried fruits soaked overnight in fruit juice or water. Cut into chunks and thread on to straws as for fresh fruit.

Citrus Fruit Salad

Serves 3–4

> *3 medium oranges*
> *1 large eating apple*
> *2 tangerines or mandarins, peeled*
> *4 oz (100 g) seedless grapes, halved*

Squeeze the juice from one orange and pour into a bowl. Peel the remaining oranges, cut off the pith with a sharp knife and cut into bite-sized pieces. Peel, core and chop the apple. Break the tangerines or mandarins into segments. Place all the fruit in the bowl with the orange juice and stir to combine.

Home-made Custard

Makes about ½ pint (300 ml)

> *½ pint (300 ml) milk (whole, semi-skimmed or skimmed)*
> *2 eggs*
> *1–2 tsp (5–10 ml) sugar or honey (optional)*
> *few drops of natural vanilla essence*

Warm the milk until fairly hot. Whisk together the eggs, sugar or honey, if using, and vanilla. Pour in the milk and stir well. Strain into a small, heavy-based saucepan and cook over a *very* gentle heat, stirring continuously, until the custard thickens. Do not let the custard boil. (If it becomes lumpy, sieve it.)

Baked Egg Custard

Serve warm as an accompaniment to stewed fruit or other desserts, or chill in the refrigerator and serve cold with slices of fresh fruit or canned fruit in fruit juice.

Serves 4

1 pint (568 ml) milk (whole, semi-skimmed or skimmed)
3 eggs
1 tbsp (15 ml) sugar

Warm the milk in a saucepan until hot but not boiling. Gently whisk together the eggs and sugar in a bowl. Pour on the hot milk, stirring well. Strain the mixture into a lightly greased oven-proof dish and bake in the oven at 170°C (325°F) mark 3 for about 40 minutes or until set in the middle and firm to the touch.

Home-made Natural Yogurt

If you do not have a yogurt maker, this yogurt can be made just as easily in a wide-necked vacuum flask. Use unpasteurised natural yogurt (most varieties in the supermarket chill cabinet are suitable). Fresh or long-life whole, skimmed or semi-skimmed milks all give good results.

Makes about 1 pint (600 ml)

1 pint (568 ml) milk
2 tbsp (30 ml) natural yogurt
3–4 tbsp (45–60 ml) skimmed milk powder

Reserve 4 tbsp (60 ml) of the milk and heat the rest to blood temperature (about 37°C/98.4°F). Blend together the reserved milk, yogurt and milk powder, then gradually stir into the warm milk. Rinse out a clean vacuum flask with boiling water, then pour in the milk mixture and screw on the lid. Leave for about 8 hours or until set. Turn into a bowl, cover and chill in the refrigerator.

Variation
Fruit Yogurt Make the yogurt as above, then flavour with chopped fresh fruit, canned fruit in fruit juice (drained), fresh fruit purée or chopped, soaked dried fruits.

Fresh Orange Jelly

High in vitamin C, this real fruit jelly is popular with children of all ages. Apple, grape or other pure fruit juices (but not pineapple) can be used instead of orange juice.

Makes about ¾ pint (450 ml)

> *4 tsp (20 ml) powdered gelatine*
> *1 tbsp (15 ml) clear honey (optional)*
> *¾ pint (450 ml) orange juice*

Put 3 tbsp (45 ml) water in a heatproof bowl, sprinkle on the gelatine and leave for about 10 minutes or until spongy. Stand the bowl over a pan of hot water and stir until dissolved. Add the honey, if using, and stir well. Add the gelatine mixture to the orange juice and stir well. Transfer to a bowl or mould, cover and chill in the refrigerator until set.

Fun Food

Pour the jelly mixture into individual novelty jelly moulds. Decorate with pieces of fruit before serving.

Apple and Yogurt Jelly

Serves 4

> *4 tsp (20 ml) powdered gelatine*
> *¾ pint (450 ml) apple juice or a mixture of apple and orange*
> *juice*
> *¼ pint (150 ml) Greek-style or low-fat natural yogurt*
> *1 eating apple*
> *lemon juice*

Put 4 tbsp (60 ml) water in a heatproof bowl, sprinkle on the gelatine and leave for about 10 minutes or until spongy. Stand the bowl over a pan of hot water and stir until the gelatine dissolves. Stir together the gelatine mixture, apple juice and yogurt and pour into a serving bowl or individual pots or bowls. Chill until set. Core the apple and cut into slices. Dip the slices in lemon juice and use to decorate the jelly.

Chunky Fruit Jelly

Use any combination of fresh fruit (but not pineapple) or canned fruit in fruit juice, drained. Clean yogurt pots can be used to make individual jellies for young children and for packed lunches, picnics or parties.

Serves 4

¾ pint (450 ml) unset Fresh Orange Jelly (page 124)
1 apple, peeled and chopped
1 banana, peeled and sliced
2 oz (50 g) seedless grapes, halved

Put a layer of fruit in the base of a shallow dish, or individual bowls or pots. Pour over the jelly and refrigerate until set.

Banana Ice-cream

Serves 4

2 large bananas, peeled
2 tsp (10 ml) honey or sugar (optional)
¼ pint (150 ml) Greek-style strained natural yogurt (made from cow's milk)
banana slices, to decorate

Mash the bananas with the honey or sugar, if using. Stir in the yogurt and mix well until smooth. Transfer to a plastic freezer container, cover and freeze until slushy. Beat well to distribute ice crystals, then freeze until set. Put the ice-cream in the refrigerator for about 30 minutes before serving to allow to soften slightly. Serve in small bowls decorated with banana slices.

Baked Bananas

This quick and easy pudding can be cooked in the oven or on a barbecue.

Serves 4

> *4 medium bananas, peeled*
> *2 tsp (10 ml) polyunsaturated margarine*
> *4 tsp (20 ml) lemon juice*
> *ground cinnamon (optional)*
> *Greek-style natural yogurt, to serve*

Place each banana on a rectangle of kitchen foil. Slice lengthways and dot with a little margarine. Sprinkle with a little lemon juice and a good pinch of cinnamon, if liked. Wrap up the bananas to form parcels and bake in the oven at 190°C (375°F) mark 5 for about 20 minutes. Serve hot, topped with a little yogurt.

Blackcurrant Mousse

Serves 4–6

> *1 lb (450 g) fresh or frozen blackcurrants*
> *1–2 oz (25–50 g) sugar or honey (optional)*
> *1 tbsp (15 ml) powdered gelatine*
> *8 fl oz (225 ml) Greek-style natural yogurt*
> *2 egg whites*

Cook the blackcurrants in a little water until soft. Stir in the sugar or honey, if using, then leave to cool. Put 2 tbsp (30 ml) water in a heatproof bowl. Sprinkle on the gelatine and leave for 10 minutes or until spongy. Stand the bowl over a pan of hot water and stir until the gelatine dissolves. Stir together the gelatine mixture, blackcurrants and yogurt, then rub through a sieve or purée in a blender or food processor. Whisk the egg whites until stiff and fold into the blackcurrant mixture. Pour into a serving dish or individual bowls and chill until set.

Fruity Rice Pudding

Serves 4

6 oz (175 g) short grain brown rice
2 oz (50 g) sultanas
1½ pints (900 ml) milk (whole, semi-skimmed or skimmed)
knob of polyunsaturated margarine
1–2 tbsp (15–30 ml) sugar or honey (optional)
a little freshly grated nutmeg
stewed fruit, to serve (optional)

Put the rice and sultanas in a 2 pint (1.1 litre) ovenproof dish. Put the milk and margarine in a saucepan and bring to the boil. Stir in the sugar or honey, if using, and pour over the rice. Sprinkle with grated nutmeg and bake in the oven at 150°C (300°F) mark 2 for about 2 hours or until the rice is tender. Serve with stewed fruit, if liked.

Blackberry and Apple Charlotte

Serves 4

8 oz (225 g) cooking apples, peeled, cored and sliced
8 oz (225 g) fresh or frozen blackberries
1–2 tbsp (15–30 ml) sugar (optional)
5 oz (150 g) wholemeal breadcrumbs
1 tbsp (15 ml) polyunsaturated margarine

Stew the apples and blackberries together in a small amount of water. Add the sugar, if necessary. Place a layer of fruit in the base of a 1 pint (600 ml) deep pie dish and sprinkle with some of the breadcrumbs. Repeat these layers, finishing with a layer of breadcrumbs. Dot with margarine and bake in the oven at 190°C (375°F) mark 5 for about 30 minutes or until the top is crisp and golden.

Kissel (Mixed Fruit Dessert)

Choose two or more fruits, such as blackcurrants, raspberries, apricots, rhubarb, cherries, plums, peaches or strawberries.

Serves 4

> *1 lb (450 g) mixed fruit*
> *2 tbsp (30 ml) arrowroot*
> *¼ pint (150 ml) water*
> *a little honey (optional)*

Prepare the fruit: Remove stones and cut larger fruit, like rhubarb, into bite-sized pieces. Blend the arrowroot with a little of the water and place in a saucepan. Stir in the remaining water and add the fruit. Bring to the boil and simmer gently for about 5 minutes or until the fruit is soft. Remove from the heat, add a little honey to taste, if liked, then cool and chill until lightly set.

Fruit Crumble

Serves 4

> *2 oz (50 g) polyunsaturated margarine*
> *4 oz (100 g) plain wholemeal flour or a mixture of wholemeal and plain white flour*
> *1 oz (25 g) sugar*
> *1 lb (450 g) prepared fruit (eg. sliced apples, rhubarb, gooseberries or plums)*

Rub the margarine into the flour until the mixture resembles fine breadcrumbs. Stir in the sugar. Place the fruit in a shallow ovenproof pie dish. Spoon the crumble mixture evenly over the fruit and press down gently. Bake in the oven at 200°C (400°F) mark 6 for 40–45 minutes or until the fruit is soft. Serve hot or cold.

Variation

Dried Fruit Crumble Use 8 oz (225 g) dried fruit instead of fresh fruit. Soak overnight in fruit juice or water and chop larger fruits into small pieces.

Strawberry Fool

Serves 2–3

> 4 oz (100 g) strawberries, hulled
> ¼ pint (150 ml) chilled Home-made Custard (page 122)
> ¼ pint (150 ml) Greek-style natural yogurt or sugar-free
>   strawberry yogurt

Chop the strawberries. Combine the custard and yogurt and stir in the strawberries. Pour into individual cartons or dishes and chill for about 30 minutes before serving.

Stuffed Peaches

Serves 2–4

> 2 oz (50 g) seedless raisins
> 3 tbsp (45 ml) apple or orange juice
> 2 oz (50 g) wholemeal sponge cake, made into crumbs
> 2 fresh peaches, stoned and halved or 4 canned peach halves
>   in fruit juice, drained
> ¼ pint (150 ml) Greek-style natural yogurt or set low-fat
>   peach yogurt (preferably sugar-free)

Soak the raisins in the fruit juice overnight until plump. Stir in the cake crumbs. Place the peaches, rounded-side down, in individual serving dishes. Spoon some of the raisin mixture into the centre of each peach half. Top each with a little yogurt and serve immediately.

Citrus Cheesecake

This tangy cheesecake is a healthy alternative to the fat- and sugar-laden varieties sold in the shops. Use sugar-free muesli and organic fruit, if possible. Otherwise, wash the skins really well.

Serves 8–10

3½ oz (90 g) polyunsaturated margarine
7 oz (200 g) muesli
1 medium orange
1 lemon
1 tbsp (15 ml) powdered gelatine
8 oz (225 g) low-fat soft cheese or curd cheese
¼ pint (150 ml) Greek-style natural yogurt
2–3 tbsp (30–45 ml) clear honey
2 egg whites
fresh fruit, to decorate (eg. orange segments, apple slices
dipped in a little lemon juice, grapes or strawberries)

Melt the margarine in a saucepan and stir in the muesli. Place in a lightly oiled loose-bottomed 8 inch (20.5 cm) cake tin and press down firmly and evenly.

Finely grate the rinds of the orange and lemon and reserve. Squeeze out the juice into a heatproof bowl and make up to ¼ pint (150 ml) with water. Sprinkle the gelatine over the juice mixture and leave for 5 minutes or until spongy. Stand the bowl over a pan of hot water and stir until the gelatine dissolves. Cool slightly.

Beat together the cheese, yogurt, honey and grated citrus rinds. Stir in the gelatine mixture. Whisk the egg whites until stiff and fold into the cheese mixture. Pour the mixture on top of the muesli base and smooth the surface. Cover and refrigerate for several hours or until set.

Run a knife around the edge of the tin to loosen the cheese-cake, then remove it from the tin. Decorate with fresh fruit.

Dried Fruit Salad

Serves 4

12 oz (350 g) mixed dried fruits (eg. apricots, pears, prunes,
apple rings, seedless raisins) or dried fruit salad
¼ pint (150 ml) apple juice
low-fat or Greek-style natural yogurt, to serve (optional)

Place the dried fruit in a large bowl, cover with boiling water and leave to soak overnight. Drain off the water and cut larger pieces of fruit into bite-sized chunks. Place in a saucepan with the apple juice, bring to the boil and simmer gently for about 10 minutes or until the fruit is tender. Allow to cool, then serve with yogurt, if liked.

Variation

Hot Fruit Salad Stir a good pinch of ground cinnamon or ginger into the fruit salad and serve while still hot.

Baked Stuffed Apples

Serves 4

> 4 medium cooking apples
> 4 oz (100 g) dried fruit (eg. sultanas, seedless raisins or chopped no-soak apricots)
> 4 tbsp (60 ml) apple or orange juice or water
> ½ oz (15 g) polyunsaturated margarine (optional)

Core the apples and make a shallow cut through the skin round the middle of each one. Stand them in a shallow ovenproof dish, fill the centres with dried fruit and pour a little fruit juice or water into each apple. Top with a small knob of margarine if liked. Cover loosely with foil and bake in the oven at 200°C (400°F) mark 6 for about 45 minutes or until the apples are soft.

Popcorn

Serve this sugar-free popcorn on its own or with a few bite-sized pieces of dried fruit.

Serves 2

> 3 tbsp (45 ml) polyunsaturated oil
> 2 oz (50 g) popcorn kernels

Heat half the oil in a large heavy-based saucepan over a fairly high heat. Add half the popcorn, *cover* and cook, shaking the pan continuously, until the kernels have popped. Remove from the pan and repeat with the remaining oil and popcorn. Cool before serving.

Fresh Fruit Trifle

This trifle can be made with one fruit or a mixture of seasonal fruits, or canned fruits in natural juices.

Serves 6–8

> *6–8 oz (175–225 g) Wholemeal Sandwich Cake (page 143)*
> *3 oz (75 g) pure fruit spread*
> *¼ pint (150 ml) apple juice*
> *10 oz (275 g) prepared fresh fruits (eg. sliced peaches, apples,*
> *   pears, bananas, halved seedless grapes, strawberries or*
> *   raspberries) or canned fruit in fruit juice, drained*
> *1 pint (600 ml) Home-made Custard (page 122), cooled*
> *slices of fruit or finely chopped nuts, to decorate*

Cut the cake into thin slices, spread with the fruit spread and use to line the base of a serving dish. Pour the apple juice evenly over the cake and leave for a few minutes or until absorbed. Spread the prepared fruit over the cake base and top with custard. Chill well and decorate with slices of fruit or chopped nuts just before serving.

Fruity Cones

It is difficult to find ice-cream cones made without sugar and additives, but at least the filling in these makes them preferable to ordinary ice-cream-filled cornets.

Makes 4

> *6 oz (175 g) apple purée*
> *2 oz (50 g) raspberry or blackberry purée*
> *sugar or honey, to taste (optional)*
> *1½ tsp (7.5 ml) powdered gelatine*
> *1 egg white*
> *4 ice-cream cones*

Mix together the puréed fruits and sweeten with a little sugar or honey, if necessary. Put 2 tbsp (30 ml) cold water in a small heatproof bowl and sprinkle on the gelatine. Leave to stand for about 10 minutes or until spongy. Stand the bowl over a pan of hot water and stir until the gelatine dissolves. Pour the gelatine mixture into the fruit and stir well. Whisk the egg white until stiff and fold into the fruit. Refrigerate until set. Scoop into ice-cream cones and serve immediately.

Fruity Yogurt Ice Lollies

Unlike ordinary lollies, these refreshing home-made fruity lollies are free from added sugar and contain no artificial additives. Make them with any pure fruit juice and fruit yogurt (sugar-free if possible) or natural yogurt. Use either lolly moulds or small cartons – the amount of juice and yogurt you need depends on the size of the moulds.

Pour some fruit juice into moulds or cartons. Put a lolly stick in position in each and freeze. When frozen, add a layer of yogurt and freeze. Add a final layer of fruit juice and freeze. To unmould the ice lollies, dip the moulds or cartons in hot water for a few seconds.

Banana Ice Pops

Nothing could be simpler to make than these frozen bananas.

Makes 4

4 small bananas

Peel the bananas and slice off a piece from one end. Push a lolly stick into the sliced end of each banana. Freeze for several hours or until firm.

HEALTHY BAKING

Home-made bread is inexpensive to make and has a delicious flavour and texture. Use the basic dough for making loaves, rolls, pizza bases or novelty shapes (see page 136) for your children. If you have a freezer, it's worth making up a larger quantity of dough and batch-baking. Some bread-making flours contain additives, so check the list of ingredients if you want to avoid them, and use organic flour or unbleached flour whenever possible.

There's no need to ban cakes and biscuits altogether, but it is worth making them as healthy as possible when your child does have them. Shop-bought cakes and biscuits tend to be high in saturated fat, sugar and additives and low in fibre. The advantage of making them yourself is that healthier ingredients can be used and you know exactly what they contain. The recipes here are made with healthy ingredients, such as wholemeal flour and polyunsaturated margarine, and sugar is kept to a minimum.

Wholemeal Bread

Makes three 2 lb (900 g) loaves

*3 lb (1.4 kg) strong plain wholemeal flour, or a mixture of
    wholemeal and srong plain unbleached white flour
1 tbsp (15 ml) sugar
1½ pints (900 ml) warm water
2 oz (50 g) fresh yeast or ½ oz (15 g) dried yeast
1 tbsp (15 ml) salt
2 tbsp (30 ml) polyunsaturated oil
cracked wheat or sesame or sunflower seeds, to
    decorate (optional)*

Place the flour in a large mixing bowl. Dissolve 1 tsp (5 ml) sugar in ½ pint (300 ml) of the water and blend in the fresh yeast or sprinkle over the dried yeast. Leave the yeast mixture in a warm place for about 15 minutes or until frothy.

Add the remaining sugar and the salt to the remaining water and stir until dissolved. Make a well in the centre of the flour and pour in the yeast, water and oil. Mix quickly to form a firm dough, adding a little more warm water if necessary. Turn on to a floured board and knead until elastic and no longer sticky. Return to the bowl, cover with a clean cloth and leave to rise in a warm place until doubled in size.

Turn the dough on to a floured board and knead briefly. Divide into three equal portions. Shape and place each piece in a 2 lb (900 g) loaf tin. Brush with water or milk and sprinkle with cracked wheat, or sesame or sunflower seeds, if liked. Cover with a cloth and leave in a warm place until the dough has risen to the tops of the tins.

Bake the loaves in the oven at 230°C (450°F) mark 8 for 25–30 minutes or until the loaves sound hollow when tapped on the bottom. Turn out and leave to cool on a wire rack.

Fun food

Give your child a little dough to make her own mini-loaves or shapes. Prove as above and bake for about 15 minutes.

Bread Animals

Children love helping to make these jolly animal rolls. Make them with some of the dough when you're baking bread, or use a packet mix. Filled with a sweet or savoury filling, they are perfect for teatime, picnics, parties and packed lunches.

Makes about 8 animals

> 1 packet brown bread mix or ¼ quantity Wholemeal Bread dough (page 134)
> beaten egg or milk, to glaze

If using a packet mix, make up, prove and knock back according to the directions on the packet. If using home-made dough, allow to rise once, knock back and proceed as follows. Divide the dough into equal pieces and shape into animals. Use a sharp knife to mark features like scales or mouths. Make features like ears, eyes and noses from tiny scraps of dough and attach to the animal's body by brushing with a little milk or water. Currants can also be used for features. Place on a baking sheet and allow to rise until doubled in size. Brush gently with beaten egg or milk and bake in a preheated oven at 220°C (425°F) mark 7 for about 15 minutes or until golden brown. Leave to cool on a wire rack.

Crocodile Shape a piece of dough into a sausage. Slightly flatten one end for the head and pinch the opposite end into a point to form the tail. Use sharp-pointed scissors to snip the dough to resemble scales on the crocodile's back. Mould the feet and eyes from scraps of dough and attach to the body. After baking, split the mouth of the crocodile open and push in a tiny piece of carrot as a tongue.

Teddy Bear Make the body and head from balls of dough. (The head should be roughly half the size of the body.) Tuck the head slightly under the body. Form a tiny snout, mouth, eyes, ears and paws from scraps of dough and attach to the body. Snip fingers, toes and a tummy button with sharp scissors.

Snakes Roll the dough between your hands into a long snake shape. Use a sharp knife to mark segments on the snake's back and curve the body in different directions so it looks wiggly. Use a tiny piece of dough or currant for an eye. After baking, push a tiny piece of raw carrot into the head to resemble a tongue.

Snail Make as for a snake, but coil up the tail to form the snail's shell.

Mouse Roll the dough into a ball, then shape one end into a point for the head. Make eyes, nose and mouth from dough and attach to the body. Make tiny feet and a tail and tuck them slightly under the mouse's body.

Bread Sticks

These miniature bread sticks are popular with children of all ages. They are ideal as healthy snacks or for serving with dips, soups or salads.

Makes about 16

> *8 oz (225 g) strong plain wholemeal flour, or a mixture of*
> *wholemeal and strong plain unbleached white flour*
> *pinch of salt*
> *⅓ sachet easy-blend yeast*
> *½ tsp (2.5 ml) sugar*
> *¼ pint (150 ml) warm water*
> *1 tsp (5 ml) polyunsaturated oil*
> *beaten egg or milk, to glaze*
> *sesame seeds*

Put the flour, salt and yeast in a bowl. Dissolve the sugar in the water and add to the flour mixture with the oil. Mix to a soft dough, adding a little more water if necessary. Turn on to a floured surface and knead for 3–5 minutes or until smooth.

Divide the dough into 16 equal pieces and roll each one into a sausage shape about 6 inches (15 cm) long. Place on oiled baking sheets, brush with egg or milk and sprinkle with sesame seeds. Cover and leave to rise in a warm place for about 20 minutes, then bake in the oven at 200°C (400°F) mark 6 for about 15 minutes or until crisp and golden.

Quick Cheese Bread

The texture of this speedy bread is similar to scones.

Makes one 1 lb (450 g) loaf

> *8 oz (225 g) self-raising wholemeal flour*
> *1 tsp (5 ml) salt*
> *1 tsp (5 ml) dried parsley or mixed herbs (optional)*
> *3 oz (75 g) Cheddar cheese, grated*
> *1 egg, beaten*
> *¼ pint (150 ml) water*
> *1 oz (25 g) polyunsaturated margarine, melted*

Mix together the flour, salt and herbs, if using. Stir in the cheese, egg, water and melted margarine and mix well. Pour into a 1 lb (450 g) loaf tin and bake in the oven at 190°C (375°F) mark 5 for 40–45 minutes or until risen and golden. Cool on a rack.

Wholemeal Scones

Makes about 10

> *8 oz (225 g) plain wholemeal flour, or a mixture of*
>   *wholemeal and plain unbleached white flour*
> *4 tsp (20 ml) baking powder*
> *1 oz (25 g) polyunsaturated margarine*
> *1 tbsp (15 ml) sugar (optional)*
> *1 egg, beaten*
> *2–3 fl oz (50–75 ml) milk*

Heat the oven to 230°C (450°F) mark 8 and warm a baking sheet.

Sift the flour and baking powder together into a bowl, adding any bran left in the sieve. Rub in the margarine until the mixture resembles fine breadcrumbs, then stir in the sugar, if using. Make a well in the centre and add the beaten egg and enough milk to give a soft dough. Transfer to a floured surface and knead lightly.

Using floured hands, flatten the dough to about ¾ inch (2 cm) thick and stamp out rounds with a 2 inch (5 cm) cutter. Re-roll the trimmings and stamp out further rounds. Place on the warm baking sheet, brush with a little milk and bake for 10–12 minutes or until well risen and golden. Cool on a wire rack.

Variation

Sultana Scones Add 2 tbsp (30 ml) sultanas with the sugar.

Herby Cheese Scones

These savoury scones are ideal for lunchboxes and picnics – split, spread with polyunsaturated margarine and add some cress or salad.

Makes about 10

> *8 oz (225 g) plain wholemeal flour, or a mixture of*
>   *wholemeal and plain unbleached white flour*
> *4 tsp (20 ml) baking powder*
> *2 oz (50 g) polyunsaturated margarine*

1–2 tsp (5–10 ml) dried mixed herbs
3 oz (75 g) Cheddar cheese, grated
1 egg, beaten
about ¼ pint (150 ml) milk
a little extra grated cheese

Sift the flour and baking powder together into a bowl, adding any bran left in the sieve. Rub in the margarine until the mixture resembles fine breadcrumbs. Stir in the dried herbs and grated cheese, then stir in the egg and enough milk to mix to a soft dough. Turn on to a floured surface and knead lightly. Using floured hands, press out the dough into a round about ¾ inch (2 cm) thick. Cut into triangular shaped wedges and place on an oiled baking sheet. Brush the tops with milk and sprinkle with a little grated cheese. Bake in the oven at 220°C (425°F) mark 7 for 10–15 minutes or until risen and golden. Cool on a rack.

Spiced Fruit Buns

Makes about 14

1¼ lb (550 g) strong plain wholemeal flour, or a mixture of
    wholemeal and strong plain unbleached white flour
1–2 tsp (5–10 ml) ground mixed spice
½ oz (15 g) fresh yeast
1 tsp (5 ml) sugar
1 pint (568 ml) warm milk (whole, semi-skimmed or
    skimmed)
2 oz (50 g) polyunsaturated margarine
1 egg, beaten
3 oz (75 g) sultanas
1 oz (25 g) sugar
a little milk, to glaze

Mix the flour and spice together and place half of it in a large mixing bowl. Blend the yeast with the 1 tsp (5 ml) sugar and ¼ pint (150 ml) warm milk and leave in a warm place for about 15 minutes or until frothy. Add to the flour in the bowl and mix to a firm dough. Cover and leave to rise for about 30 minutes.

Dissolve the margarine in the remaining milk and add to the beaten egg.

Mix the milk mixture into the risen dough with the rest of the flour, the sultanas and sugar. Mix well and leave to rise again until doubled in size. Turn on to a floured board and knead well. With floured hands, break off pieces of dough and form into balls. Place on a well oiled baking sheet and flatten slightly. Leave until well risen, brush with milk, then bake in the oven at 220°C (425°F) mark 7 for 15–20 minutes or until golden. Cool on a wire rack. Serve warm, cold or split and toasted.

Fruit Loaf

Store this Fruit Loaf, wrapped in foil or cling film, for a few days before eating, to allow the flavour to develop.

> ¾ pint (450 ml) hot tea (ordinary or fruit tea)
> 12 oz (350 g) mixed dried fruit
> 5 oz (150 g) soft brown sugar
> 10 oz (275 g) self-raising wholemeal flour
> 1 tsp (5 ml) ground mixed spice
> 1 egg

Grease and base-line a 2 lb (900 g) loaf tin. Mix the tea, dried fruit and sugar in a bowl. Cover and leave to soak overnight.

Add the flour, spice and egg to the fruit mixture and mix well. Turn into the prepared tin and cook in the oven at 180°C (350°F) mark 4 for about 1½ hours. Turn out and cool on a wire rack. Serve in slices, plain or spread with a polyunsaturated margarine.

Fruity Bread Pudding

A healthy version of an old-fashioned favourite. Inexpensive to make, it's ideal for picnics and lunchboxes.

1 lb (450 g) bread, preferably wholemeal
1 pint (568 ml) milk (whole, skimmed or semi-skimmed)
12 oz (350 g) sultanas
4 oz (100 g) no-soak dried apricots, chopped
3 oz (75 g) soft brown sugar
1 tsp (5 ml) ground cinnamon
1 tsp (5 ml) freshly grated nutmeg
4 oz (100 g) polyunsaturated white vegetable fat, frozen
2 eggs, beaten

Cut the crusts off the bread and break into small pieces. Place in a large bowl and pour over the milk. Leave to soak for about 20 minutes. Meanwhile, grease and base-line a 3 pint (1.7 litre) roasting tin. Squeeze out the bread, reserving the excess milk, then use a fork to break up the lumps of bread. Add the sultanas, chopped apricots, sugar and spices.

Grate the frozen fat into the bread mixture and stir in quickly. Add the egg and a little of the reserved milk, if necessary, to give a dropping consistency. Pour the mixture into the prepared tin and level the top. Bake in the oven at 180°C (350°F) mark 4 for about 1½ hours or until firm to the touch. Allow to cool in the tin, then cut into slices and store in an airtight container.

Banana Bread

4 oz (100 g) polyunsaturated margarine
4 oz (100 g) soft brown or caster sugar
3 large ripe bananas
2 eggs, beaten
8 oz (225 g) plain wholemeal flour
2 tsp (10 ml) baking powder

Grease and base-line a 2 lb (900 g) loaf tin. Beat together the margarine and sugar until fluffy. Mash the bananas well, mix with the eggs and stir into the creamed mixture. Sift in the flour and baking powder, adding any bran left in the sieve. Fold the flour into the banana mixture. Pour into the prepared tin and bake in the oven at 180°C (350°F) mark 4 for about 1¼ hours or until a skewer inserted in the centre comes out clean.

Malt Loaf

This fruity malt loaf is ideal for packed lunches. Wrap and store for several days before serving, to let the flavour and texture develop.

>*12 oz (350 g) plain wholemeal flour, or a mixture of*
>   *wholemeal and plain unbleached white flour*
>*½ tsp (2.5 ml) bicarbonate of soda*
>*1 tsp (5 ml) baking powder*
>*½ tsp (2.5 ml) ground mixed spice (optional)*
>*8 oz (225 g) seedless raisins or sultanas*
>*1 oz (25 g) soft brown sugar*
>*8 tbsp (120 ml) malt extract*
>*2 eggs, beaten*
>*7 fl oz (200 ml) milk (whole, semi-skimmed or skimmed)*

Grease and base-line a 2 lb (900 g) loaf tin. Sift together the flour, bicarbonate of soda, baking powder and spice into a bowl, adding any bran left in the sieve. Stir in the raisins or sultanas.

Warm the sugar and malt extract together in a pan. Pour into the flour with the eggs and milk and beat well. Spoon into the prepared tin and bake in the oven at 150°C (300°F) mark 2 for about 1½ hours or until a skewer inserted in the centre comes out clean. Cool on a wire rack.

Apple Cake

>*8 oz (225 g) plain wholemeal flour*
>*2 tsp (10 ml) baking powder*
>*1 tsp (5 ml) ground cinnamon*
>*4 oz (100 g) polyunsaturated margarine*
>*1 lb (450 g) cooking apples, peeled, cored and chopped*
>*2 oz (50 g) sultanas*
>*4 oz (100 g) caster sugar*
>*3 eggs, beaten*

Grease and base-line an 8 inch (20.5 cm) square cake tin. Mix the flour, baking powder and spice together in a bowl. Rub in the margarine until the mixture resembles breadcrumbs. Stir in the apples, sultanas, caster sugar and eggs. Spoon the mixture into the prepared tin and level the top. Bake in the oven at 190°C (375°F) mark 5 for about 1½ hours or until a skewer inserted in the centre comes out clean. Cool on a wire rack.

Carrot Cake

6 oz (175 g) soft brown sugar
6 oz (175 g) polyunsaturated margarine
3 eggs, beaten
10 oz (275 g) self-raising wholemeal flour
½ tsp (2.5 ml) ground cinnamon
8 oz (225 g) carrots, grated
4 oz (100 g) walnuts, finely chopped
grated rind of 1 lemon

Grease and line an 8 inch (20.5 cm) round cake tin. Cream the sugar and margarine together until fluffy, then beat in the eggs, a little at a time. Sift in the flour and cinnamon, adding any bran left in the sieve, and mix well. Stir in the grated carrots, walnuts and lemon rind.

Pour the mixture into the prepared tin, level the top and bake in the oven at 180°C (350°F) mark 4 for about 1½ hours or until a skewer inserted in the centre comes out clean. Cool slightly in the tin, then turn out and cool on a wire rack. Serve plain or spread the top with some Lemony Cheese Icing (page 149).

Wholemeal Victoria Sandwich Cake

This version of the traditional teatime cake is made with healthier ingredients, such as wholemeal flour and polyunsaturated fat. It does, however, contain quite a bit of sugar, so choose a low-sugar filling or topping.

6 oz (175 g) polyunsaturated margarine
6 oz (175 g) sugar
3 eggs, beaten
6 oz (175 g) self-raising wholemeal flour

143

Grease and base-line two 7 inch (18 cm) sandwich cake tins. Cream together the fat and sugar until pale and fluffy. Gradually add the eggs, beating well between each addition. Sift in the flour, adding any bran left in the sieve, and beat well. Divide the mixture between the prepared tins, level the tops and bake in the oven at 180°C (350°F) mark 4 for about 40 minutes or until well risen and firm to the touch. Turn out and leave to cool on a wire rack. Sandwich together with one of the following:

* Lemony Cheese Icing (page 149)

* Puréed fruit, pure fruit spread or Sugar-free Jam (page 70)

* Mashed banana (add a little lemon juice to prevent browning) or slices of fresh fruit (eg. strawberries, peaches or pears)

Apple and Date Bars

Makes 16

> 4 oz (100 g) polyunsaturated margarine
> 3 oz (75 g) soft brown sugar
> 3 tbsp (45 ml) golden syrup
> 6 oz (175 g) rolled oats
> 2 oz (50 g) plain wholemeal flour
> 1 tsp (5 ml) baking powder
> 8 oz (225 g) cooking apples, peeled, cored and chopped
> 4 oz (100 g) stoned dates, chopped

Grease a 7 inch (18 cm) square cake tin. Melt the margarine, sugar and syrup in a pan over a low heat. Stir well and cool. Mix together the rolled oats, flour and baking powder. Stir in the syrup mixture and mix thoroughly.

Spoon half the mixture into the prepared tin, spread evenly and press down well. Mix together the chopped apples and dates and spread over the oat base. Cover with the remaining oat mixture and press down firmly. Bake in the oven at 180°C (350°F) mark 4 for 25–30 minutes or until firm and golden brown. Mark into 16 bars, cool slightly in the tin, then carefully lift out and cool on a wire rack. Store in an airtight container.

Muesli Bars

These crunchy cereal bars are ideal as an occasional sweet treat or for picnics and lunchboxes. Stored in an airtight container, they will keep for up to 2 weeks.

Makes 12

4 oz (100 g) polyunsaturated margarine
4 tbsp (60 ml) clear honey
2 oz (50 g) soft brown sugar
8 oz (225 g) muesli (preferably sugar-free)
2 oz (50 g) no-soak dried apricots, chopped
2 oz (50 g) seedless raisins or sultanas

Lightly oil a 7 × 11 inch (18 × 28 cm) Swiss roll tin. Melt the margarine, honey and sugar in a pan. Stir in the muesli, apricots and raisins. Spread the mixture in the prepared tin and press down lightly. Bake in the oven at 180°C (350°F) mark 4 for 25 minutes. Cool in the tin for 10 minutes, then cut into 12 bars and transfer to a wire rack.

Gingerbread Men

Children love helping to make these funny little biscuits. Let them stamp out shapes with novelty cutters and decorate with currants.

Makes 6–8

3 oz (75 g) plain wholemeal flour
3 oz (75 g) plain unbleached white flour
½ tsp (2.5 ml) bicarbonate of soda
½ tsp (2.5 ml) ground ginger
½ tsp (2.5 ml) ground cinnamon
2 oz (50 g) polyunsaturated margarine
2 oz (50 g) caster sugar
1 tbsp (15 ml) black treacle, warmed
1 egg, beaten
currants

Sift the flours, bicarbonate of soda and spices into a bowl, adding any bran left in the sieve. Rub in the margarine and stir in the sugar. Mix together the treacle and egg and pour into the flour mixture. Mix well, then bring together into a ball and knead until smooth.

Turn the dough on to a floured surface and roll out to about ¼ inch (0.5 cm) thick. Stamp out shapes with cutters. Re-roll the trimmings and stamp out more shapes. Place on lightly oiled baking sheets and press in currants for eyes, noses and mouths. Bake in the oven at 190°C (375°F) mark 5 for 12–15 minutes. Cool slightly, then lift carefully on to a wire rack and leave to cool completely.

Oat Biscuits

Makes about 24

> 2 oz (50 g) plain unbleached white flour
> 2 oz (50 g) plain wholemeal flour
> 4 oz (100 g) rolled oats
> 2 oz (50 g) caster sugar
> 2½ oz (65 g) polyunsaturated margarine, well chilled
> 1 egg, beaten
> 2–3 tbsp (30–45 ml) milk

Mix together the flours, oats and sugar in a bowl. Rub in the margarine. Bind with the beaten egg and add enough milk to form a stiff dough. Turn on to a lightly floured surface and roll out thinly. Cut into rounds with a 2½ inch (6 cm) cutter and place on greased baking sheets. Re-roll the trimmings and stamp out more rounds. Bake in the oven at 180°C (350°F) mark 4 for about 15 minutes or until crisp and golden. Cool on a wire rack and store in airtight containers.

Cheese Straws

Makes 24

75 g (3 oz) plain wholemeal flour, or a mixture of wholemeal
and plain unbleached white flour
large pinch of mustard powder
1½ oz (40 g) polyunsaturated margarine, chilled
1½ oz (40 g) Cheddar cheese, finely grated
1 egg, beaten

Sift the flour and mustard together into a bowl, adding any bran remaining in the sieve. Rub in the margarine until the mixture resembles fine breadcrumbs, then stir in the cheese. Stir in about half the beaten egg to form a soft dough.

Turn the dough on to a floured surface and knead lightly until smooth. Roll out to a rectangle about 3 × 12 inches (7.5 × 30.5 cm), then cut into ½ inch (1 cm) strips. Carefully twist each strip and place on a greased baking sheet. Brush with beaten egg. Bake in the oven at 180°C (350°F) mark 4 for 12–15 minutes or until golden. Cool on a wire rack and store in an airtight container.

Variation

Sesame Cheese Straws Sprinkle the cheese straws with sesame seeds just before baking.

Tiny Cheese and Tomato Tarts

These little savoury tarts are just the right size for small fingers.

Makes 12

4 oz (100 g) Wholemeal Shortcrust Pastry (page 149)
2 oz (50 g) Cheddar cheese, grated
1 tomato, sliced
¼ pint (150 ml) milk
1 egg, beaten

Roll out the pastry thinly on a lightly floured surface. Cut out 12 rounds with a 2½ inch (6 cm) cutter and use to line twelve 2 inch (5 cm) patty tins. Sprinkle a little cheese into each pastry case. Cut the tomato slices in four and place a piece on top of each tart. Whisk together the milk and egg and spoon some of the mixture into each pastry case. Bake at 190°C (375°F) mark 5 for about 20 minutes or until the filling is set and beginning to brown.

Fresh Fruit Tarts

These little fruit tarts are ideal to make with leftover pastry. Vary the filling depending on which fruits are in season. If you need only one or two tarts at a time, store the remaining cooked, unfilled tarts in an airtight container or wrap and freeze until required.

Makes 6–8

> *2 oz (50 g) Wholemeal Shortcrust Pastry (page 149)*
> *small selection of fruit cut into tiny bite-sized pieces (eg.*
> *tangerine segments, seedless grapes, chopped apple,*
> *banana slices, halved strawberries or raspberries)*

Roll out the pastry on a lightly floured surface and cut out six or eight rounds with a 2½ inch (6 cm) cutter. Use to line 2 inch (5 cm) tart tins. Prick the bases with a fork and bake blind at 200°C (400°F) mark 6 for 12–15 minutes or until just beginning to brown. Allow to cool, then fill with a selection of prepared fruits. Serve immediately.

Dried Fruit Treats

These little balls made from dried fruits make a healthier alternative to sweets. Although there is no added sugar, the natural sugar in the dried fruit can still lead to tooth decay, so save them for mealtimes, lunchboxes or occasional treats.

Makes about 15

> *2 oz (50 g) no-soak dried apricots*
> *2 oz (50 g) stoned dates*
> *2 oz (50 g) sultanas or seedless raisins*
> *2 oz (50 g) finely chopped nuts (eg. walnuts, brazils or*
> *almonds)*

1 tsp (5 ml) lemon juice
sesame seeds, for coating

Soak the fruits in boiling water for 30 minutes, then drain and
pat dry. Mince or very finely chop the fruits and mix with the
nuts and lemon juice. Form into bite-sized balls and roll in
sesame seeds to coat. Store in an airtight container.

Wholemeal Shortcrust Pastry

Shortcrust pastry made with wholemeal flour and polyunsaturated fat is a healthier alternative to traditional pastry. If you
find the texture too heavy, try using half wholemeal and half
unbleached white flour.

Makes 4 oz (100 g) quantity

4 oz (100 g) plain wholemeal flour
2 oz (50 g) polyunsaturated margarine, well chilled
1½–2 tbsp (25–30 ml) cold water

Put the flour into a mixing bowl. Rub in the margarine until
the mixture resembles fine breadcrumbs. Gradually add enough
water to form a smooth dough. Wrap in cling film until required.

Lemony Cheese Icing

Use this tangy low-fat icing to fill or top cakes – the quantity
below makes enough to fill one sandwich cake. Because of the
low sugar content it should be stored in the refrigerator and
eaten within 3–4 days.

6 oz (175 g) low-fat soft cheese (not cottage cheese)
finely grated rind and juice of 1 lemon
1–2 tsp (5–10 ml) clear honey

Cream the cheese until soft and fluffy. Beat in the lemon rind,
2–3 tsp (10–15 ml) of the juice and honey to taste. Keep refrigerated until required.

SOFT DRINKS

Sooner or later your baby will need something to drink other than breast or formula milk. Babies can drink ordinary cow's milk from about 6 months, although it is better to breast or bottle feed with formula milk until a year. Follow-on milks produced for babies over 6 months have no real advantages and are an expensive way of buying milk.

Once your baby is eating a reasonable variety of foods and starts to drink less milk at feedtimes (usually around 7–8 months) you can start offering a drink of water or *well-diluted* fruit juice from a spouted cup at one meal.

Milk, water or diluted juice are the best choice for older children, too. Sugary soft drinks, like orange squash and cola, are popular with youngsters but contain few nutrients – most are little more than sugar and water and many contain additives such as colourings and preservatives. High juice squashes, with around 40 per cent juice, are the best choice if your child insists on squash, but they are still high in sugar and diluted juice is far better. Making your own soft drinks means you can avoid the high levels of sugar and additives in manufactured drinks and provide your child with some useful nutrients at the same time.

Banana Milkshake

Serves 1

> 1 small banana
> 6 fl oz (175 ml) chilled milk (whole, semi-skimmed or
>   skimmed)

Peel and slice the banana and liquidize with the milk in a blender until smooth. Serve immediately.

Dressed-Up Drinks

Cocktails and other fun-looking drinks are popular with older children and ideal for parties and special occasions.

✻ Provide a variety of fruit juices and fizzy mineral water and let the children mix their own 'cocktails'.

✻ Slices of orange or lemon and a few ice cubes transform ordinary soft drinks into something sophisticated.

✻ For fruity ice cubes, place tiny seedless grapes, cherries, raspberries, lemon slices or mint leaves in ice cube trays, top up with water and freeze. Add to drinks just before serving.

✻ Use tiny cutters to stamp out stars, hearts and other shapes from apple slices. Toss in lemon juice to prevent browning and spear on to drinking straws or add to drinks just before serving.

Lemonade

Serves 1

1–2 tsp (5–10 ml) lemon juice
¼ pint (150 ml) sparkling mineral water
slice of lemon

Stir the lemon juice into the mineral water and add a slice of lemon.

Fruit Fizz

Makes 1 pint (600 ml)

> *½ pint (300 ml) pure fruit juice (eg. apple, orange, pineapple*
> *or a mixture of juices)*
> *½ pint (300 ml) sparkling mineral water*
> *apple or orange slices (optional)*

Mix together the fruit juice and mineral water, pour into glasses and add a few slices of apple or orange, if liked.

Strawberry Milkshake

Serves 3–4

> *6 oz (175 g) strawberries, hulled*
> *¾ pint (450 ml) cold milk (whole, semi-skimmed or skimmed)*
> *¼ pint (150 ml) Greek-style natural yogurt*
> *3 strawberries, sliced, to garnish (optional)*

Mix the ingredients together and liquidize in a blender until smooth. Pour into glasses and float a few slices of strawberry on top, if liked.

Hot Fruit Punch

This warming fruity drink can be made with one fruit juice or a mixture.

Makes 1 pint (600 ml)

> *1 pint (600 ml) apple juice*
> *6 cloves*
> *small cinnamon stick*
> *1 eating apple, cored and sliced*

Put the apple juice in a saucepan with the cloves and cinnamon and heat gently until hot but not boiling. Remove from the heat, stand for a few minutes, then strain and serve in cups with a few apple slices.

HELPFUL ORGANISATIONS

The following groups and organisations offer information and advice about different aspects of, or problems related to, feeding babies and children. Remember to enclose a stamped addressed envelope with your enquiry. Telephone numbers are given for those organisations that will deal with enquiries by telephone.

General Information
The Health Education Authority
Hamilton House, Mabledon Place, London WC1H 9TX
Tel: 01–631 0930
Offers general information about healthy eating for babies and children. Some local health authorities or health education units also produce information about healthy eating.

Information and Support for Breastfeeding Mothers
The Association of Breastfeeding Mothers
10 Herschell Road, London SE23 1EG
Tel: 01–778 4769
Runs a telephone advice service for breastfeeding mothers and has a network of local groups.

La Leche League
PO Box BM 3424, London WC1N 3XX
Tel: 01–242 1278

The National Childbirth Trust
Alexandra House, Oldham Terrace, Acton, London W3 6NH
Tel: 01–992 8637
Both the above give help, advice and support to breastfeeding mothers and have a nationwide network of breastfeeding counsellors.

Help with Special Diets
The Coeliac Society
PO Box 181, London NW2 2QY
Offers help and information to parents of children medically diagnosed as having coeliac disease (intolerance to gluten) and dermatiis herpetiformis. The society produces a range of helpful literature, including a handbook which details the medical and dietary aspects of the disease and also gives recipes and a list of manufactured products which are gluten-free.

The Cystic Fibrosis Trust
5 Blyth Road, Bromley, Kent BR1 3RS
Tel: 01–464 7211
Produces useful leaflets (including nutritional management) which are free to parents of Cystic Fibrosis children and also have local groups.

The British Diabetic Association
10 Queen Anne Street, London W1M 0BD
Tel: 01–323 1531
Produces a range of helpful information for parents of diabetic children and general information for coping with a diabetic way of life.

Asthma Research Council
300 Upper Street, London N1 2XX

The National Eczema Society
Tavistock House North, Tavistock Square, London WC1H 9SR
Produces a range of booklets and leaflets explaining the condition and outlining dietary measures that help some individuals.

The Hyperactive Children's Support Group
71 Whyke Lane, Chichester, Sussex PO19 2LD
Tel: 0903–725182
Support group for parents of hyperactive children.

The National Society for Research into Allergy
PO Box 45, Hinkley, Leicester LE10 1JY

The British Kidney Patient Association
Bordon, Hampshire
Gives advice on specific dietary questions.

The National Society for Phenylketoneuria and Allied Disorders
26 Towngate Grove, Mirfield, West Yorkshire
Produces some excellent recipes and general diet information sheets, plus leaflets explaining the condition.

The Research Trust for Metabolic Diseases in Children
53 Beam Street, Nantwich, Cheshire CW5 5NF
Tel: 0270–629782
Offers advice and puts parents of children with metabolic diseases in touch with each other.

Vegetarian Diets
The Vegetarian Society UK Ltd
Parkdale, Dunham Road, Altrincham, Cheshire WA14 4QG
Tel: 061 928 0792
Publishes a range of useful leaflets, cookbooks and information about feeding vegetarian babies and children.

The Vegan Society
33 George Street, Oxford
Tel: 0865 722166
Produces recipe books and information about nutrition for vegan babies and children.

Help with Disabilities
Cleft Lip and Palate Association
Dental Department, Hospital for Sick Children, Great Ormond Street, London WC1N 3JH

Disabled Living Centre
Musgrave Park Hospital, Stockman's Lane, Belfast BT9 7JB
Information and advice on coping with disabilities including feeding equipment for the disabled.

Voluntary Council for Handicapped Children
8 Wakely Street, Islington, London EC1V 7QE
Has details of organisations offering help with specific handicaps.

Making Your Voice Heard
If you are concerned about the food your family eats, want consumers to get a better deal, or simply want to learn more about food, the following organisations are worth joining or supporting.

Both are committed to independent research and education about food, campaigning for better, healthier food and putting pressure on the government and food industry to bring about changes that will benefit consumers.

The London Food Commission
88 Old Street, London EC1V 9AR
Tel: 01–253 9513

Provides information, education and advice on all aspects of food. Produces an excellent bi-monthly magazine (*The Food Magazine*) crammed with information on all aspects of food and food policy.

Parents for Safe Food
Britannia House, 1–11 Glenthorne Road, Hammersmith, London W6 0LF

A new organisation working for safe wholesome food and committed to protecting the interests of all consumers. Produces a 'Parents' Kit' and helpful information about food and ways to go about getting the sort of food you want.

Benefits
For information about the benefits you may be entitled to (extra money, free school meals, vitamins and milk, for example), contact your local Social Security office. Alternatively, contact the Department of Health's free telephone information service who will advise about benefits – 0800 666555 (0800 616757 in Northern Ireland).

INDEX